Botanica's
100 Best
BULBS

FOR YOUR GARDEN

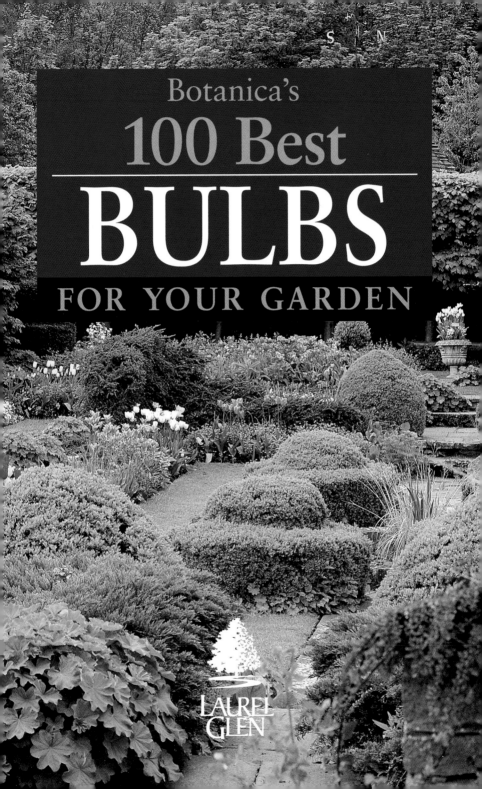

Botanica's
100 Best
BULBS
FOR YOUR GARDEN

LAUREL
GLEN

First published in 2001 in North America by
Laurel Glen Publishing
An imprint of the Advantage Publishers Group
5880 Oberlin Drive, San Diego, CA 92121–4794
www.advantagebooksonline.com

Text © Random House Australia Pty Ltd 2001
Photos © Random House Australia Pty Ltd 2001
from the Random House Photo Library

All notions of errors or omissions should be addressed to
Laurel Glen Publishing, editorial department, at the above
address. Other correspondence (author inquiries, permissions
and rights) concerning the content of this book should be
addressed to Random House Australia, 20 Alfred Street,
Milsons Point, NSW 2061

Library of Congress Cataloging-in-Publication Data

Botanica's 100 best bulbs for your garden
    p. cm.
    ISBN 1-57145-478-0
    1.Bulbs. I. Title: Botanica's one hundred best bulbs for
your garden. II. Laurel Glen Publishing.

SB425 .B595 2000
635.9'4--dc21   00-052155

1 2 3 4 5 01 02 03 04 05

Publisher: James Mills-Hicks
Managing editor: Susan Page
Editor: Jane Warren
Publishing assistant: Anabel Pandiella
Consultant: Geoff Bryant
Page makeup: Southern Star Design
Production manager: Linda Watchorn
Film separation: Pica Colour Separation, Singapore
Printed by: Dah Hua Printing Co. Ltd, Hong Kong

PHOTOGRAPHS, COVER AND PRELIMINARY PAGES

Cover:
Tulipa cultivars (front)

Hyacinthus orientalis (back)

Page 1:
Ranunculus cultivars

Pages 2-3:
Sedum, Erica, Begonia, Aster and *Tulipa* cultivars

Pages 4-5:
Tulipa cultivars

Pages 6-7:
Narcissus cultivars

CONTENTS

INTRODUCTION

The term "bulbs" encompasses a large group of plants whose common characteristic is their ability to form underground storage organs, usually in the form of modified stems, leaves or roots. These organs, known as (true) bulbs, rhizomes, corms or tubers, not only provide nutrition for the plant during a period of dormancy, but are also the means by which these plants reproduce.

A true bulb, such as the tulip or daffodil, hyacinth and snowdrop, is essentially an underground bud on a greatly reduced stem, and the modified leaves that cover the bulb are the storage organs.

Tulipa, Darwin Hybrid, 'Oxford's Elite'

Bulbs may be either tunicated (like daffodils) or "naked" or scaly (like lilies), depending on the arrangement of the leaves covering the bulb. Naked bulbs are more susceptible to drying out.

A corm is an underground stem that is swollen to form a storage organ covered in scale leaves. *Gladiolus*, *Crocus* and *Montbretia* are corms. After dormancy the terminal bud formed at a node produces a new corm that can be separated from the parent plant.

A tuber, too, is a swollen underground stem that has scale leaves and buds, known as "eyes," from which the new plants arise. The best example of tuberous plants are Dahlias.

A rhizome is a swollen stem that grows horizontally on, or just below, the soil surface. Lateral buds developing in the axils of the scale leaves form branch rhizomes that can be separated from the parent plant. Irises and *Agapanthus* are rhizomatous plants; the rhizomes of *Agapanthus* grow vertically, however, and are known as root stocks.

Although they are frequently

associated with spring color—the *Crocus* and daffodil are the true harbingers of spring in the Northern Hemisphere—in fact there is a bulb for every month of the year, and their range of flower colors and form is quite dazzling. Bulbs vary in size from the tiny snowdrop and *Crocus* to 10 ft (3 m) giants. Bulbs occur wild in a variety of habitats, such as woodland, meadow, alpine and waterside, and most of these conditions can be approximated in the garden.

Bulbs are quite inexpensive and readily available and, given some simple care and attention, they will reward the novice and experienced gardener alike with showy displays, often year after year.

Use in the garden

Bulbs are some of the most versatile plants available to us, and their use in the garden reflects this. Most can be grown in the flower garden or in containers, both indoors and outdoors, and even, in the case of summer-flowering bulbs, in mixed herbaceous borders. Bulbs such as *Gladiolus*, *Galtonia*, *Eucomis* and many alliums are especially useful in a border planting, where they add both height and vivid color. Lilies, too, are excellent in borders, but their extravagant blooms and sweet fragrance may be more fully appreciated when they are planted in containers. Many bulbs can be successfully naturalized under trees or in the lawn, where they thrive on "neglect" and improve their display year on year.

The secret to harnessing the full potential of bulbs lies in the careful planning of a year-round display; the selection and purchase of good quality bulbs; and the timely planting and appropriate care of the chosen bulbs.

Choosing the best position to plant bulbs is important, but particularly so for spring-flowering bulbs. Decide on the position from within the house: that way, you can ensure that the flowers are visible from the comfort of the home, and you do not need to venture out into the cold or wet to enjoy them. Alternatively, plant them alongside a well-trodden path, or near the front door. Most bulbs do well in an open, sunny site, with well-drained soil, and it is always a good idea to prepare and feed the soil in preparation to planting.

In general, bulbs will look at their best if you try to emulate their natural growing conditions. Woodland bulbs, for example, such as bluebells, snowdrops and cyclamens, will do well beneath deciduous trees, while those that favor meadows, like daffodils, crocuses and snake's head fritillary, often flower early and need a little more sun. These bulbs naturalize successfully in lawn or grassy orchards and will die back before the grass begins to compete with them.

Growing habits and effects

Bulbs look best when planted in groups of 3, 5 or 7, rather than in rows or formal plantings. Bulbs naturalized under trees or in lawn—if left undisturbed—will seed themselves and increase in number by underground offsets, so that every year the drifts of color will be bigger and better. In either situation, the best effect is created when you plant the bulbs informally. A simple way of achieving this "natural look" is to face away from the planting site, toss the bulbs over your shoulder, and plant them where they fall.

Although naturalizing bulbs in lawn is a popular planting method,

Agapanthus Species

it is worth noting that the lawn should be left unmown after the bulb has flowered, to allow time for the leaves to die down and replenish the underground food store, ready for next year. For daffodils, this period is at least 6 weeks. If your lawn is a formal feature of the garden, therefore, it may be best to avoid this method of bulb display.

Whereas it is often difficult to establish herbaceous perennials under deciduous trees and shrubs, which is the garden equivalent of the edge of a wood, naturalized woodland bulbs will thrive in this setting. Here, they enjoy a dry, dormant period in summer, while in spring, they receive a comfortable amount of light and rainfall. Once established, bulbs growing under trees need very little maintenance: leaves shed by the trees in autumn keep them well fed.

Alpine bulbs, such as dwarf daffodils, crocuses and anemones, and the more tender bulbs, such as cannas, agapanthuses and ixias, will need to be grown under cover. Alpine bulbs suit raised beds, with gritty, well-drained soil, and need protection from wet. The tender bulbs should be overwintered and protected from frost in cold areas. Depending on the climate, some tender bulbs can be planted out in spring; others will need to be housed permanently in the greenhouse or conservatory.

Many bulbs do well in indoor and outdoor containers. Deep containers are ideal: there should be 2–4 in (5–10 cm) of soil above, and 8–10 in (20–25 cm) below, the bulb. The principal advantage of growing bulbs in containers is that they can be moved into view at the point of flowering, and they can be turned to ensure even growth. Lilies make superb container specimens, but are particular about their growing conditions: they like cool roots, so place in a shady spot, or grow a ground cover in the same pot.

Dahlia, Group 4, 'Emanuel Friediirkeit'

Starting out... and getting results

When buying bulbs, select large, firm, heavy specimens, preferably from cultivated (rather than wild) stock. Reject any that have signs of damage to the neck or base, those that are shooting, and those with evidence of disease, such as surface discoloration. Roots should be short and thick, and the tunics of tunicated bulbs (like tulips, narcissi and hyacinths) should be intact. Garden centers stock popular bulbs, but a wider variety is available through mail order.

Plant bulbs as soon as possible after purchase. If a delay is unavoidable, store them in netting bags or paper bags—never in plastic bags. Lilies, however, should be planted immediately, or kept in peat or a peat substitute until you are ready to plant them. When planting in lawn, either lift a section of turf, plant a group of bulbs and replace the turf, or use a special bulb planter to cut individual, bulb-sized holes.

Time the planting of your bulbs to maximize their potential. Plant winter-, spring- and early summer-flowering bulbs in autumn, and plant summer-flowering bulbs at the end of spring.

The correct depth depends on the type of bulb, but as a rule of thumb, most bulbs should be planted at a depth at least twice or three times their height. Space them out to avoid overcrowding and failure to flower.

Which way up? Make sure that you plant the bulb the right way up, with the pointed shoot at the top, and the rounded base and roots at the bottom. Some bulbs, like begonias and gloxinias, can be difficult to orient correctly.

Keep the soil moist while the bulbs are actively growing, and water container bulbs regularly. Good drainage is essential for bulbs grown in containers. Place a layer of crocks or broken pot shards at the base of the container and use a soil-based compost with added grit.

A regular feed of a high-potash fertilizer is advisable for most bulbs. **After flowering,** nip off the flower stem of daffodils and tulips to arrest seed development, but allow naturalized bulbs to set seed. Leave the foliage of all bulbs to die back naturally (with the exception of rhizomatous plants, which need to be cut back) and don't bother to knot the foliage of narcissus—this practice serves no purpose.

Propagate bulbs by dividing well-established clumps, usually in late summer to autumn (for late autumn-, winter- and spring-flowering bulbs) or in spring (for summer- and early autumn-flowering bulbs). Propagation from seed takes longer, but can be rewarding.

Pests and diseases are specific to the type of bulb, but some, like mice, slugs, snails, cutworm, eelworm and vine weevil, are common to all. Aphids, thrips and bulb flies may also be a nuisance. Fungal disease may be caused by overcrowding, over-watering and poor air circulation around plants.

Wash your hands after handling bulbs: some bulbs, like tulips and hyacinths, act as an irritant to skin, and bulbs may have been treated with fungicide.

Tulipa cultivars dominate this mixed border.

AB

AGAPANTHUS

African lily, agapanthus,
lily-of-the-Nile

Native to southern Africa, these strong-growing perennials are popular for their fine foliage and imposing flowers produced in abundance over summer. Arching, strap-shaped leaves spring from short rhizomes with dense, fleshy roots. Flowers are assorted shades of blue (some cultivars are white) in many flowered umbels, borne on a long erect stem, often reaching 3 ft (1 m) or more tall. Agapanthuses are ideal for background plants or for edging along a wall, fence or driveway. Some hybrid examples are '**Irving Cantor**' and '**Storm Cloud**'; **Headbourne Hybrids** are especially vigorous and hardy. They grow to 3 ft (1 m) and come in a range of bright colors.

CULTIVATION *Agapanthus* can thrive in conditions of neglect, on sites such as dry slopes and near

Agapanthus 'Irving Cantor'

Agapanthus africanus

the coast. They enjoy full sun but will tolerate some shade, and will grow in any soil as long as they get water in spring and summer. They naturalize readily, soon forming large clumps; they also make excellent tub and container specimens. Remove spent flower stems and dead leaves at the end of winter. Agapanthuses are frost

Agapanthus campanulatus

hardy to marginally frost hardy. Propagate by offsets or division in late winter, or from seed in spring or autumn.

Agapanthus africanus

From the Western Cape Province of South Africa, this species is moderately frost tolerant. It produces flowers on 12–24 in (30–60 cm) stems from midsummer to early autumn; each flowerhead contains 20 to 50 individual blossoms, the color varying from pale to deep violet blue. Often plants sold under this name turn out to be *Agapanthus praecox*. The most obvious difference between the two species is the length of the leaves; *A. africanus* having much shorter leaves than those of *A. praecox*. **'Albus'** is a lovely, award-winning cultivar. ZONES 8–10.

Agapanthus campanulatus

Native to KwaZulu Natal in South Africa, this species forms a large clump of narrow, grayish leaves that die back in autumn. In mid- to late summer, crowded umbels of pale blue flowers with broadly spreading petals are borne on 3 ft (1 m) stems. It is the most frost-hardy agapanthus. *Agapanthus campanulatus* var. *patens*, smaller and more slender, is one of the daintiest of all the agapanthus. ZONES 7–11.

ALLIUM

This is a large genus consisting of more than 700 species of bulbous perennials and biennials that occur in temperate regions of the Northern Hemisphere and range in height from 4 in–5 ft (10 cm–1.5 m). Some species are edible, including onions, garlic and chives. Common to the genus is the oniony smell emitted when the leaves are bruised or cut. All species have flowers in an umbel terminating on a small, erect stalk and sheathed in bud by membranous bracts. Bulbs can be very fat or quite slender but generally produce new bulbils at the base, sometimes also in the flower stalks.

CULTIVATION They prefer a sunny, open position in fertile, well-drained, weed-free soil. Watch for onion fly, stem eelworm, rust and onion white rot. Propagation is either from seed or bulbils.

Allium caeruleum
syn. *Allium azureum*

This frost-hardy species from central Asia has very short, narrow leaves which wither by the time its 12–24 in (30–60 cm) flowering stalks have fully lengthened. These bear dense umbels of starry blue flowers in summer. ZONES 6–9.

Allium christophii
syn. *Allium albopilosum*
Star of Persia

Growing to 24 in (60 cm), this species has broad leaves, green and shiny on top and white beneath, and the sturdy stem bears a rounded umbel of flowers up to 15 in (38 cm) wide in spring. Star-shaped individual violet flowers turn black as the seeds ripen and are useful for dried flower arrangements. Plant bulbs in autumn, $2\frac{1}{2}$ in (6 cm) deep. This species grows best in full sun. ZONES 7–9.

Allium giganteum
Giant allium

Among the tallest of the flowering alliums, this species has 4–6 ft (1.2–1.8 m) stems topped with dense, 4–6 in (10–15 cm) diameter

Allium giganteum

Allium 'Purple Sensation'

umbels of violet to deep purple flowers in midsummer. The leaves are gray-green, 18 in (45 cm) or more long. **'Purple Sensation'** is rather similar to *Allium giganteum*, from which it may possibly be derived, differing in the deep rosy purple of its 3 in (8 cm) diameter spherical heads, which are carried on 3 ft (1 m) stems. ZONES 6–10.

Allium karataviense

The most striking feature of this spring-flowering species from central Asia is the 2–3 broad, flat leaves that spread widely from the base, dull gray-green in color, flushed with purple. The short flowering stems terminate in dense umbels of star-shaped white to pale purple flowers, their petals with darker central veins. The name is a latinization of Kara Tau, the mountain range in Kazakhstan where the species was first found. ZONES 3–9.

Allium karataviense

Allium moly

Allium moly
Golden garlic

Native to southern Europe, in some parts of which its appearance in a garden was regarded as a sign of prosperity, *Allium moly* grows to 15 in (45 cm). Broad, gray-green basal leaves surround stems, each bearing an umbel of up to 40 flowers. The brilliant yellow, star-shaped flowers appear in summer. "Moly" was the classical

Useful Tip

When lifting bulbs or corms remember to save the tiny offsets. They may take a year or two to flower, but they will all be true to type.

name of a magical herb, fancifully applied to this species by Linnaeus. ZONES 7–9.

ALSTROEMERIA

Peruvian lily

Native to South America where they occur mostly in the Andes, these tuberous and rhizomatous plants with about 50 species are among the finest perennials for cutting, but they do drop their sepals. Erect, wiry stems bear scattered, thin and twisted leaves concentrated on the upper half, and terminate in umbels of outward-facing flowers, usually with flaring petals that are variously spotted or streaked. Peruvian lilies flower profusely from spring to summer.

CULTIVATION All grow happily in sun or light shade in rich, well-drained acidic soil. They soon form large clumps, bearing dozens of flowerheads. Propagate from seed or by division in early spring. They are frost hardy, but in cold winters protect the dormant tubers by covering with loose peat or dry bracken. Best left undisturbed when established, but one-year-old seedlings transplant well. Alstroemerias do well naturalized under trees or on sloping banks.

Alstroemeria haemantha

Alstroemeria haemantha
Herb lily

This Chilean species has green leaves with a slightly hairy margin. The stiff flower stems, growing to 3 ft (1 m) tall, carry up to 15 orange to dull red flowers during early summer, their upper petals splashed with yellow. The plants can spread by their fleshy rhizomes to form quite large patches. ZONES 7–9.

Alstroemeria, Ligtu Hybrids

The well-known Ligtu Hybrids first appeared in Britain in the late 1920s, when *Alstroemeria ligtu* was crossed with *A. haemantha*. They come in a range of colors from cream to orange, red and yellow, but have been overshadowed in recent years as cut flowers by other hybrid strains derived from *A. aurea*. The plants die down soon after flowering. ZONES 7–9.

Alstroemeria, Princess Series

Developed by Peter Smith of Chactonbury Nursery, by royal appointment, these English hybrids are heavy flowering compact plants that are now available in a wide color spectrum. The flowers last

Alstroemeria, Ligtu Hybrid

well when cut. Plant them in late spring in moist, well-drained soil and incorporate a heavy dressing of peat or well-rotted manure. 'Princess Victoria', 'Diana Princess of Wales', 'Princess Frederika', 'Princess Beatrix' and 'Queen Elizabeth the Queen Mother' are just some of the more popular cultivars. ZONES 7–9.

AMARYLLIS

This genus contains some of the most beautiful of all flowering bulbs. Linnaeus' concept of *Amaryllis* was in fact a mixed one, including the American plants we now know as *Hippeastrum* as well as the familiar South African belladonna lily. As now recognized, the genus consists of a single species, occurring wild only in Western Cape Province. Its notable feature is the way its long-stemmed umbels of lovely rose-pink flowers appear in late summer and early autumn from leafless bulbs, the bright green, rather succulent leaves emerging after the flowers wither. Occasionally grown are generic hybrids between *Amaryllis* and related genera: best known are × *Amarcrinum* (with *Crinum*) and × *Amarygia* (with *Brunsvigia*). CULTIVATION Plant large bulbs in late summer at soil level or

just below, in well-drained soil. A fairly sunny position is best in cool areas, but they may need light shade in very warm areas. Cut down flower stalks once flowering is finished but ensure the plant is well watered through winter. Grown easily from seed, it often self-sows freely.

Amaryllis belladonna
syn. *Callicore rosea*
Belladonna lily

This plant is a gardener's dream— moderately frost hardy, easy to grow and, as the name *belladonna* implies, it is quite beautiful. A very sturdy, fast lengthening stem up to 30 in (75 cm) high is topped with a glorious display of rosy pink, lily-like flowers about 4 in (10 cm) long.

Amaryllis belladonna

Amaryllis belladonna 'Hathor'

The strap-like basal leaves appear in a large clump after the long flowering period. Over a number of years the bulbs can multiply to form a clump up to 24 in (60 cm) or so in width. There are many cultivars, including the free-flowering **'Johannesburg'** with pale pink flowers; **'Hathor'** with large, white flowerheads; and **'Kimberley'** which has deep carmine flowers with white throats. ZONES 8–11.

ANEMONE

Windflower

This genus of over 100 species of perennials occurs widely in the Northern Hemisphere, with the majority in temperate Asia. Species include a diverse range of woodland plants as well as the common florist's anemone *(Anemone coronaria)*. All have tufts of basal leaves that are divided in palmate fashion into few to many leaflets. The starry or bowl-shaped flowers have 5 or more petals, in almost all flower colors. Tuberous and rhizomatous anemones, which include the ground-hugging *A. blanda* and *A. nemorosa,* are usually spring flowering. There are rhizomatous species which tolerate less moisture and prefer conditions that are more open. Given the right conditions and left undisturbed for a number of years, many of these plants will form wonderful carpets of both leaf texture and color through their delicate flowers. Tuberous-rooted anemones, of which *A. coronaria* is best known, flower in spring and are best replaced every year or every other year.

CULTIVATION Most woodland species are very frost hardy and do well in rich, moist yet well-drained soil in a lightly shaded position. Propagate from seed planted in summer or divide established clumps in early winter when the plants are dormant. The tuberous-rooted types appreciate full sun, a well-drained soil and a dry dormancy period.

Anemone blanda 'White Splendour'

However, these anemones are prone to frost damage and the tubers tend to become weakened after blooming, so they are most often treated as annuals.

Anemone blanda

This delicate-looking tuberous species is frost hardy. Indigenous to Greece and Turkey, it grows to 8 in (20 cm) with crowded tufts of ferny leaves. White, pink or blue star-shaped flowers, $1\frac{1}{2}$ in (35 mm) wide, appear in spring. It self-seeds freely and given moist, slightly shaded conditions, should spread into a beautiful display of flowers. 'White Splendour', as its name suggests, bears large, beautiful white flowers in spring; 'Charmer' produces deep pink blooms; 'Pink Star' has bright pink flowers; and 'Radar' bears white-centered magenta flowers. ZONES 6–9.

Anemone blanda 'Radar'

Anemone coronaria, De Caen Group

Anemone coronaria

Wind poppy, florist's anemone

This very frost hardy species, the most commonly planted anemone, is one that dies back to small woody tubers; these are sold in packets just like seeds, the plants being treated almost as annuals. They grow to about 10 in (25 cm) high, and the poppy-like flowers, up to 4 in (10 cm) wide, can range in color from pink to scarlet, purple or blue; they are excellent for cutting. The two best known strains are the **De Caen** and **St. Brigid Groups**, with single and double flowers respectively, and colors ranging from purple to pink to scarlet to blue. Examples of the former are 'The Bride' with white flowers; 'Mr. Fokker' with deep blue flowers; and the bright red 'Hollandia'. In the St. Brigid Group, white 'Mount Everest' and the deep pink 'The Admiral' are fine forms. ZONES 8–10.

Anemone nemorosa

Anemone nemorosa
Wood anemone

As its common name implies, this European species is happiest in a moist, shaded position where its delicate creamy white, spring to early summer flowers delight passersby. Usually under 4 in (10 cm) high, *Anemone nemorosa* has fine creeping rhizomes that will quickly cover an area if conditions are suitable. Many named cultivars exist, including '**Allenii**', a rich lilac blue on the outside of the petals and pale lilac on the insides; '**Robinsoniana**', with lavender-blue petals; and '**Vestal**', a late-blooming white variety. ZONES 5–9.

Anemone coronaria, St. Brigid Group

ARISAEMA

Jack in the pulpit

This genus of the arum family consists of around 150 species of

Anemone nemorosa 'Robinsoniana'

Arisaema sikokianum

tuberous or rhizomatous perennials found in temperate to tropical parts of the Northern Hemisphere. Their foliage is variable and they often have only one or two leaves per shoot. The leaves are usually divided, sometimes very finely, and make a frilled base to the erect, flowering stem that emerges through the center of the foliage. The flowering stems vary in height depending on the species, and carry a single flower spike in spring or early summer. The bloom has a central spadix of minute, fleshy flowers surrounded by a greenish spathe. Size, color and shape of the spathe varies widely. Heads of fleshy red fruit follow the flowers.

CULTIVATION Most of the cultivated species tolerate moderate to severe frosts and prefer to grow in woodland conditions with cool, moist, humus-rich soil and dappled shade. Propagate from seed or offsets.

Arisaema sikokianum

This Japanese native is probably the most widely cultivated species. Its flower stem is around 18 in (45 cm) tall and it has 2 trifoliate leaves with leaflets up to 6 in (15 cm) long. The spathe is 6–8 in (15–20 cm) long, deep purple on the outside with a stark white interior. The spadix is also pure white with an upright, club-shaped appendage. ZONES 7–9.

ARUM

Many plants are called arums, however only a few truly belong to this genus. All are worth growing, but only two or three are widely available. They are tuberous perennials with broad, fleshy leaves, usually arrowhead-shaped and often variegated with a paler green along the veins. The true flowers are minute, carried in the finger-like spadix that terminates the thick flower stalk; the spadix in turn is encircled by the more conspicuous spathe, or bract.

CULTIVATION The more leafy species, such as *Arum italicum,* are easily grown in part shade in moist but well-drained, humus-rich soil, and require no attention. Propagate by division after the foliage dies back, or from seed in autumn.

Arum italicum
Italian arum

Growing to 12 in (30 cm), this species has broad, arrow-shaped, green leaves marbled white in autumn. Appearing in early spring, the flower spike has a light green, hooded spathe with an erect yellow spadix in the center. It is followed by orange berries that last until late summer. ***Arum italicum* subsp. *albispathum*** has plain green leaves;

Arum italicum

'**Marmoratum**' has contrasting pale green to cream marbling. ZONES 7–10.

BEGONIA

There are over 1,500 known species of *Begonia* from around the world. They range from rhizomatous perennials a few inches (centimeters) high to 10 feet (3 meter) shrubs. Many begonias are grown indoors, prized for their beautifully colored and textured foliage or showy flowers,

Begonia, Tuberhybrida Group, Illumination Series

sometimes both present on the one species or cultivar. Mostly evergreen, their broad, usually asymmetrical leaves have a somewhat brittle and waxy texture.

Useful Tip

For an early show, plant pots of spring bulbs in late summer, plunge them in the garden, then lift and bring them indoors in midwinter.

Female flowers, as distinct from male flowers that are on the same plant, have broad, colored flanges on the ovaries, which develop into winged fruits.

The rhizomatous begonias are a large and varied class, with leaves arising directly from creeping, knotty rhizomes—they include **B. rex**, parent of the Rex-cultorum begonias with colorfully variegated leaves. Tuberous begonias are now generally represented by hybrids of the Tuberhybrida Group, which die back to tubers in winter and bear large, showy, often double flowers in summer. **CULTIVATION** The tuberous begonias need special treatment: tubers must be forced into growth in early spring at a temperature of 65°F (18°C) in peat moss or sphagnum, and kept in a cool, well-ventilated greenhouse for the summer flowering season. After flowering, the plants die back and tubers are lifted around the middle of autumn and stored dry. Propagate from tubers.

Other begonias may be propagated from stem or leaf cuttings (laying the cut leaf blades flat on damp sand and weighing them down with pebbles), or by division of rhizomes, or from seed. Begonias are susceptible to mold and mildew in the warmer part of the year if conditions are too damp.

Begonia, Tuberhybrida Group

The glorious large blooms come as singles or doubles, with many variations of frills and ruffles, in almost every color except blues.

Begonia, Tuberhybrida Group, Acaena cultivar

Begonia, Tuberhybrida Group

These hybrids are derived from a number of South American species. In midspring the tubers sprout, producing weak, brittle stems up to 24 in (60 cm) long with rather sparse, mid-green leaves. The summer flowers can weigh down the stems, which may need staking. After flowering, plants enter their dormant stage and the tubers are normally lifted in midautumn and stored dry. Several subgroups are recognized, based on growth form and flower type. Most numerous are the **Camellia-flowered** and **Rose-flowered** cultivars, with very large, mostly double flowers up to 6 in (15 cm) across or even larger, in the full range of colors (examples are **'Fairylights'** and **'Mandy Henschke'**); their multiplicity of petals develop only in the male flower when the smaller

Begonia, Tuberhybrida Group, 'Fairylights'

B., Tuberhybrida Group, 'Mandy Henschke'

single female flowers that grow on either side of the central male are removed. **Picotee Group** cultivars are mostly double blooms with petal edges washed in contrasting or deeper shades of the flower color. Cultivars of the **Multiflora** type, are in the main, single-flowered and are grown mainly for their effect *en masse*: available in the same color range and grown in the same way as the others, they need no bud removal.

Begonia, Tuberhybrida Group, Picotee Type

Plants can be floppy and will benefit from staking. The **Pendula Group** carry their flowers in pendent sprays; known sometimes as "basket begonias," they look best cascading from hanging baskets. The single or double flowers are usually smaller than Camellia- or Rose-flowered types but come in the same color range and grow in the same way. ZONES 9–11.

BERGENIA

Consisting of 6 or 7 species of rhizomatous, semi-evergreen perennials of the saxifrage family from eastern and central Asia, this genus is characterized by large, handsome, paddle-shaped leaves, arising from the ground on short stalks to form loose clumps. There are also many garden hybrids that have been developed over the last 100 years or so. Large clusters of flowers—mostly pale pink, but also white and dark pink—are borne on short, stout stems in winter and spring. An example is **'Eroica'**, with deep pink flowers. The foliage often develops attractive red tints in winter.
CULTIVATION Bergenias thrive in sun or shade and tolerate exposed sites as well as moist

Bergenia × schmidtii

ground beside streams or ponds. Leaves color most strongly when plants are grown under drier conditions. Some are good as ground cover when planted *en masse*. Water well in hot weather and remove spent flowerheads to prolong flowering. Propagate by division in spring after flowering, when plants become crowded.

Bergenia × schmidtii

Arguably the most vigorous and most widely planted bergenia, this old hybrid between *Bergenia ciliata* and *B. crassifolia* has large, rounded, fleshy, dull green leaves. Set among the foliage are dainty rose-pink blooms on stalks growing to 12 in (30 cm) long. The main flush of flowers occurs in late winter and early spring; frosts may damage the delicate blooms, but it often flowers sporadically at other times. The plant spreads to make a fine ground cover, and adapts well to warm-temperate humid climates. ZONES 5–10.

C

CALLA

Bog arum

This genus, a member of the arum family, consists of a single species found in cool-temperate regions of the Northern Hemisphere. It is a semi-aquatic, deciduous or semi-evergreen perennial that grows in the boggy margins of lakes and swamps. It has thick rhizomes and long-stalked, smooth, heart-shaped leaves in a loose clump. The inflorescences are typical of the arum family, with a broad, rather flat white spathe and a short central spadix of very small fleshy cream flowers, which develop into closely packed small red fruits. The plants often called "calla lilies" are in fact the African *Zantedeschia aethiopica*, not to be confused with the true genus *Calla*.

CULTIVATION The water arum does best in boggy soil and will flourish when planted in up to 10 in (25 cm) depth of still or slow-moving water. While full sun is best, some shade in warmer areas is tolerated. Propagation is either by division in early spring, or from seed sown in pots and then barely submerged in water. It will often self-seed if conditions are favorable.

Calla palustris

This plant grows to about 12 in (30 cm) high, and the dark green glossy leaves are up to 8 in (20 cm) long. The white spathes, similar in shape to the upper stem-clasping leaves, are flushed with green and appear through summer. Old spathes persist beneath the clustered heads of bright red berries. ZONES 2–9.

CAMASSIA

Camas, quamash, beargrass

This genus of North American lilies consists of 5 or more species, some divided into many subspecies and varieties, ranging in the wild from British Columbia to California and Utah. They

---

Useful Tip

A little sand or fine grit at the bottom of the planting hole improves drainage and can deter some bulb-feeding pests.

---

grow in moist meadows in very large numbers and the edible bulbs, like rather gummy potatoes when boiled, were a very important food item of the indigenous people. From the midst of rather coarse leaf tufts rise the flower stems, studded along their length with clear blue, white or purple stars.

CULTIVATION Very frost hardy and easily grown in most temperate climates, the bulbs should be planted in late autumn in well-drained, loamy, humus-rich soil. Position in part-shade, or full sun if the soil is very moist. Propagate by division or from seed; the latter may take up to 5 years to produce flowers.

Camassia quamash
syn. *Camassia esculenta*
Camash, swamp sego

This, the most important edible species, is also a fine ornamental. It occurs over a wide area of southwestern Canada and northwestern USA. The flowering stems are 12–36 in (30–90 cm) tall and are densely covered with 1–2 in (25–50 mm) wide, star-shaped, pale to deep blue flowers in spring and early summer. A very variable species, eight subspecies are recognized. *Camassia quamash* var. *brevifolia* has duller, more gray-green leaves and flowers that are a deeper shade of blue-violet. *C. quamash* 'Orion' has larger racemes of dark blue flowers. ZONES 4–9.

Camassia quamash var. *brevifolia*

CANNA

This genus of robust rhizomatous perennials consists of about 25 species, native to tropical and South America. Their apparent aboveground stems are not true stems but collections of tightly furled leaf bases, rising from the thick, knotty rhizomes. Slender flowering stems grow up through the centers of these false stems, emerging at the top with showy flowers of asymmetrical structure. Most of the wild species have rather narrow-petaled flowers in shades of yellow, red or purple. Garden cannas, on the other hand, are hybrids with much broader petals. Colors range from red, orange and yellow through to apricot, cream and pink. The leaves can be green, bronze or purple, or sometimes white or yellow striped. Plants range in height from 18 in (45 cm) to 8 ft (2.4 m).

CULTIVATION Cannas thrive outdoors in frost-free, warm climates. In colder areas the roots need to be protected with thick mulch in winter, or lift the rhizomes in autumn and store until spring—alternatively they can be grown in containers in a conservatory or greenhouse. Aphids and red spider mite can prove to be a problem when plants are grown in a conservatory. Cut back to the ground after flowering finishes. Propagate in spring by division.

Canna × generalis

Canna × *generalis* is a large, highly variable group of canna hybrids of unknown or complex parentage. Plants are extremely variable, ranging from dwarfs of less than 3 ft (1 m) to large growers that reach 6 ft (1.8 m). Foliage is also variable and may be plain green, reddish, purple or variegated. Flowers come in all the warm shades, either in

Canna × *generalis* cultivar

Canna × *generalis*

plain single colors like the orange-red **'Brandywine'** or spotted or streaked as in the yellow and red **'King Numbert'**. **'Königin Charlotte'** has dazzling red flowers.

'Lucifer' is a most attractive hybrid with yellow-edged red petals and purple-toned leaves. It is a dwarf type, growing to about 3 ft (1 m). ZONES 9–12.

Canna × *generalis* 'Brandywine'

Canna × *generalis* 'Königin Charlotte'

Canna × generalis 'Lucifer'

CARDIOCRINUM

Knowing the derivation of a plant's name may enable us to picture the plant itself and *Cardiocrinum* is a good example: made up from the Greek "kardia," meaning heart, and "krinon," a type of lily, its leaves are heart-shaped and the magnificent flowers are lily-like. This genus includes 3 species from cool-temperate regions of eastern Asia, all of which are monocarpic (the plant dies after flowering); however, many offsets are produced.

CULTIVATION These plants like deep, moist, well-drained, nutrient-rich soil. Plant bulbs in autumn just below the soil surface, ensuring there is ample room between bulbs for best effect. Water and fertilize well once the shoots appear. Although the main bulb dies after flowering, propagation is possible from off-sets (which flower in 3 or 4 years) and seed. Buying 3 sizes of bulbs will ensure some flowers appear each year. Snails and slugs can be a problem.

Cardiocrinum giganteum
syn. *Lilium giganteum*
Giant lily

Native to mountains of central and western China, this is a magnificent, summer-flowering plant

Cardiocrinum giganteum

reaching up to 12 ft (3.5 m). This is a plant for the patient gardener: the giant lily does not produce quick results—a small bulb planted today is unlikely to flower in less than 3 or 4 years. The tall, sturdy stem bears up to 20 trumpet-shaped flowers, each about 10 in (25 cm) long; they are creamy white, striped maroon in the throat and are heavily scented. ZONES 6–9.

CHIONODOXA

Glory-of-the-snow

These small bulbs are relatives of the hyacinth. There are 6 species in the genus, restricted in the wild to mountains of southern Turkey, Crete and Cyprus; they are all desirable garden plants. Plant them in quantity to show off the wonderful clarity of the rich blue flowers with their white centers; lilac-pink flowers are also available. The flowers appear in late winter or early spring, depending on climate.

CULTIVATION They need full sun or light shade, well-drained soil and cold winter temperatures; in warmer climates they will languish and often fail to initiate flower-buds. Propagate from seed or offsets.

Chionodoxa forbesii
syn. *Chionodoxa luciliae* of gardens, *C. siehei*

From the rugged mountains of southwestern Turkey, this is the most widely grown species but has generally been misidentified as *Chionodoxa luciliae* in bulb catalogues. The plants are up to about 8 in (20 cm) high with broad, strap-shaped, fleshy leaves appearing with the flowers. The flowering stems can each carry up to 12 flowers, about $^3/_4$ in (18 mm) across, of a very bright violet-blue except for the whitish center. '**Alba**' has pure white flowers. '**Pink Giant**' has pink flowers with white centers and grows to 8–10 in (20–25 cm) tall. ZONES 4–9.

Chionodoxa forbesii

Chionodoxa luciliae 'Alba'

Chionodoxa luciliae
syn. *Chionodoxa gigantea*

Native to the same region of Turkey as *Chionodoxa forbesii*, this species resembles it in many respects but has only two to three flowers per stem and each flower has slightly broader, softer lilac petals and a smaller white central spot. **'Alba'** has all-white flowers. ZONES 4–9.

Chionodoxa sardensis

Sardes is a classical place-name from southwestern Turkey and "sardensis" is the Latin adjective referring to it. This species also comes from much the same region as *Chionodoxa forbesii*, and is a fairly similar plant but with narrower,

more channeled leaves. The flowers are gentian-blue with a white eye, up to 12 per stem. ZONES 4–9.

CLIVIA

Kaffir lily

This genus of southern African lilies was named after Lady Clive, Duchess of Northumberland, whose grandfather was the famous Clive of India. She was a patron of gardening and *Clivia nobilis* first flowered in the UK in her greenhouses. The genus consists of 4 species of evergreen perennials with thick, strap-like, deep green leaves springing from short rhizomes with thick roots. Flowers are borne in dense umbels terminating somewhat flattened stems and are funnel-shaped to trumpet-shaped, with 6 red to orange, sometimes green-tipped petals that are partially fused into a tube. They are sometimes followed by quite conspicuous, deep red, berry-like fruits. CULTIVATION They will grow well outdoors in a mild, frost-free climate, or in a conservatory or greenhouse in regions with colder climates. Plant in a shaded or part-shaded position in friable, well-drained soil. They are surface rooting, however, and dislike soil disturbance. Keep fairly dry in

Clivia miniata

winter and increase watering in spring and summer. Propagate by division after flowering. Clivias may also be grown from seed, but can be slow to flower.

Clivia miniata

Bush lily, fire lily

This most commonly cultivated and showiest species is distributed widely in eastern South Africa. About 18 in (45 cm) in height, it has broad leaves, sometimes up to 3 in (8 cm) wide, and bears clusters of broadly funnel-shaped flowers up to 3 in (8 cm) long, mostly orange to scarlet with a yellow throat, usually in spring but with the occasional bloom at other times. Many cultivars have been selected over the years, including yellow and cream forms. There is a group of especially prized hybrids with tulip-shaped, deep, rich scarlet blooms. ZONES 8–11.

Clivia miniata (yellow form)

COLCHICUM

Autumn crocus

Colchicum consists of about 45 species, native to Europe, North Africa and west and central Asia. Despite the name "autumn crocus," they bloom in either spring or autumn, depending on species. All have flowers with a very long tube, the ovary at or below soil level, the petals spreading at the top into a usually narrow funnel; they have 6 stamens. With few exceptions the leaves appear after the flowers and are mostly broad and fleshy. All parts of the plants are poisonous and contact with the skin may cause irritation— the poisonous compound colchicine is used in the treatment of certain forms of cancer, and in plant breeding.

CULTIVATION Frost hardy, they are easy to grow as long as winters are sufficiently cold. Some of the Mediterranean species like hot, dry summer conditions and need a warm spot in the rock garden with good drainage. Plant corms in late summer in well-drained soil in full sun or part-shade. Corms can be flowered once without any soil, so they can be kept inside for display. Propagate from seed or by division of the corms in summer.

Colchicum autumnale

Autumn crocus, meadow saffron

This best known species comes from Europe. The goblet-shaped

Colchicum autumnale

Colchicum autumnale 'Album'

flowers rise 4–6 in (10–15 cm) above the ground. Appearing from late summer to midautumn, they vary a little in color but are usually a delicate shade of lilac pink. This is one of the most moisture tolerant species, and the one occurring furthest north. '**Album**' has white flowers and '**Alboplenum**' has double white flowers. ZONES 5–9.

COMMELINA

A widespread genus of about 230 species of perennial herbs from tropical and subtropical regions of the world, related to *Tradescantia*. They vary in growth habit, some species sending up erect annual growths from tuberous roots, others with more evergreen and usually creeping stems which root at the nodes. Their distinctive features are the asymmetrical boat-shaped bract that encloses each group of flowerbuds, and the three petals of which often only two are conspicuous, each narrowed at the base into a fine "claw." Many *Commelina* species have petals of an intense, clear blue, though pinks and whites are also known.

Commelina coelestis

CULTIVATION A position in full sun is preferred and a well-drained soil is essential. In colder climates, lift the tubers and store until spring. Propagate from cuttings or by division.

Commelina coelestis
Mexican dayflower

Native to Central and South America including Mexico, this species has vivid sky-blue flowers that close in the afternoon, each with 3 equal petals and about 1 in (25 mm) across. They open in late summer and autumn. The weak, semi-erect stems with broad green leaves spring from a deep, tuberous rootstock and may reach a height of 3 ft (1 m). It needs a warm position in full sun. 'Alba' produces white flowers. ZONES 9–11.

CONVALLARIA

Lily-of-the-valley

Some botanists have recognized several species of *Convallaria*, but most believe there is only one, occurring wild in forests from France to Siberia, and cooler parts of North America. The plant spreads over the forest floor by slender underground rhizomes which at intervals send up pointed oval leaves and slender flowering stems adorned with little white bells, shining like pearls against the dull green of the foliage. The red berries that follow have their uses in medicine, but they are extremely poisonous.

CULTIVATION The rhizomes should be planted in autumn in a part-shaded position. Given the right conditions it spreads freely, and in a confined space may become overcrowded; it will then benefit from lifting and thinning. Grow in fertile, humus-rich,

Useful Tip

Bulbs need water too. If the winter has been dry, water spring bulbs as the flower buds appear. Summer bulbs need routine watering. Autumn-flowering bulbs can stay dry until midsummer.

moist soil. Lily-of-the-valley can be potted for display indoors, then replanted outdoors after flowering. Propagate from seed or by division.

Convallaria majalis

Renowned for its glorious perfume, this beautiful plant does best in cool climates. It is low growing, 8–12 in (20–30 cm) high but of indefinite spread, with mid-green leaves. The dainty white bell-shaped flowers, $\frac{1}{4}$–$\frac{1}{2}$ in (6–12 mm) across, appear in spring. Pink-flowered variants are collectively referred to as *Convallaria majalis* var. *rosea*, and there are several

Convallaria majalis

cultivars with variegated or gold foliage. 'Fortin's Giant' is a tall vigorous form; 'Prolificans' bears panicles that resemble inflorescences; and 'Variegata' has attractively striped foliage. ZONES 3–9.

CORYDALIS

The 300 or so species in this genus, allied to the fumitories *Fumaria*), occur in temperate regions of the Northern Hemisphere. Mostly perennials, but with some annuals, their basal tufts of ferny, deeply dissected leaves spring from fleshy rhizomes or tubers. The smallish tubular flowers, with a short backward-pointing spur that may be curved, are usually in short spikes. They are mostly creams, yellows, pinks and purples; a few have clear blue flowers. **CULTIVATION** The sun-loving species do well in rock gardens,

Convallaria majalis var. *rosea*

while the shade lovers are best planted beneath border shrubs or in a woodland garden. Soil should be moist but well drained, and rich in humus for woodland species. Several species self-seed freely. Propagate either from seed or by division.

Corydalis cava
syn. *Corydalis bulbosa*

From central Europe, this is an early spring-flowering, tuberous perennial 4–8 in (10–20 cm) high. The epithet "cava" means "hollow" and refers to the tuber and stem base, which are hollow. The species is unusual in having no basal leaves but only two smallish, dissected leaves on each erect stem, which terminates in a crowded spike of pale purple to white flowers about 1 in (25 mm) long with short, curved spurs. It tends to die down in summer. ZONES 6–9.

Corydalis flexuosa

This species forms a small clump of green foliage around 12 in (30 cm) tall. In late spring and early summer, short spikes of long-spurred, tubular, clear blue flowers, each about 1 in (25 mm) long, appear above the foliage. It requires a cool spot in part-shade and moist soil. 'Pere David' has intense blue flowers; 'Purple Leaf' is prized for its bronze purple new-season's growth. ZONES 5–9.

Corydalis flexuosa

CRINUM

The bulbs of this genus are often quite large and may be deeply buried or sit virtually on the soil surface; in many species the bulb is elongated with a "neck" of varying length on which the old dead leaf bases persist as papery sheaths. The lily-like flowers are borne in umbels at the apex of thick flowering stems and usually open progressively; usually white or pink, they have six broad petals, often upward-curving, and long stamen filaments. Globular, thin-skinned fruits contain large fleshy seeds that have no dormancy and will begin to germinate dry. Only a few species and 2 or 3 hybrids are widely grown in gardens.

CULTIVATION Plant bulbs in rich, moist soil with the neck of the bulb above ground level. Some species do best in full sun, others appreciate a light shade. Propagation is best from seed as dividing the plants is difficult. The flowers usually take a few seasons to develop with either method. Most species are tender to frost and susceptible to slugs, caterpillars and snails.

Crinum moorei
Moore's crinum, bush lily

This cold-hardy crinum is popular for the delicate beauty of its large white to pale pink flowers. The very broad, weak leaves are usually beginning to die back as the flowers open in late summer and early

Crinum moorei (white form)

Crinum moorei 'Cape Dawn'

autumn, finally leaving a clump of large, very long-necked bulbs protruding above the ground. Flowering stems reach up to 3 ft (1 m) tall, and are topped by umbels of 4–5 in (10–12 cm) wide nodding flowers of very graceful appearance. It prefers a friable, well-drained soil; it is prone to damage from snails and slugs. '**Cape Dawn**' is a delicate pink form. ZONES 8–11.

Crinum × powellii
Cape lily

This easily grown hybrid between *Crinum bulbispermum* and *C. moorei* was bred in England in the nineteenth century. Strap-like foliage is produced from a long neck and dies back during late summer and

autumn. At about the same time the 3–4 ft (1–1.2 m) flowering stems are each crowned with up to 10 deep pink, fragrant flowers, similar in shape and size to those of *C. moorei*. The flowers can become so heavy that the plant needs to be staked. '**Album**' has pure white flowers. ZONES 6–10.

Crinum × powellii 'Album'

CROCOSMIA

syn. *Antholyza, Curtonus*
Montbretia

These 7 species of South African cormous perennials have narrow, bayonet-shaped, pleated leaves. These fan out from the base of the plant, similar to a gladiolus. A branched spike of brightly colored flowers is produced in summer.

CULTIVATION Plant the corms in winter in rich soil with good drainage in a position that gets the morning sun. Water well through summer. They will multiply freely and should not be divided unless overcrowded; if necessary, divide in spring.

Crocosmia × crocosmiiflora

Growing to 36 in (90 cm), the stem of this hybrid bears a branching spike of up to 40 orange-red, gladiolus-like flowers about 1 in

Crocosmia × crocosmiiflora 'Lucifer'

(25 mm) wide. Although frost hardy, it needs full sun in cold climates. In cold-winter areas, lift the corms and replant in spring. Larger flowered hybrids in a wider range of colors (yellow to red) are also available, including the bright orange-red '**Bressingham Blaze**' and '**Lucifer**' (bright red). '**Jackanapes**' has mid-green leaves and bears bicolored flowers in yellow and orange-red in late summer. '**Hamilton**' bears golden

Crocosmia × crocosmiiflora

yellow flowers with apricot centers;
'Star of the East' has clear orange
flowers with pale orange centers
and it reaches 30 in (75 cm).
ZONES 7–11.

Crocosmia masoniorum

This species grows up to 4 ft
(1.2 m) tall. The branched stem is
topped with an arched display of
tangerine flowers. The 6-petaled
flowers are quite large, up to 3 in
(8 cm) wide. **'Walberton Red'**
was the result of several years'
crossing between *Crocosmia
masoniorum, C. pottsii* 'Solfatare'
and 'Her Majesty' by D. R. Tristram
of Arundel in West Sussex. It has
uplifted large flowers of a pure
tomato-red color. The corms are

Crocosmia masoniorum 'Walberton Red'

also large and do not split into a
mass of cormlets. ZONES 8–11.

Crocosmia masoniorum

CROCUS

This genus of cormous perennials has goblet-shaped flowers that taper at the base into a long tube that originates below the soil surface. Crocuses vary greatly in color, though lilac-blue, mauve, yellow and white are most usual. Spring-flowering species and hybrids bear flowers with or before the new leaves; autumn-flowerers bloom in full leaf. The foliage is grass-like, usually with a central silver-white stripe.

CULTIVATION Very frost-hardy, crocuses do best in cool to cold areas. In warmer areas, they can be grown in pots in a cool spot. Plant corms in early autumn in moist, well-drained soil in full sun or part-shade. Divide clumps if they are overcrowded. Seed can

Crocus chrysanthus 'Dorothy'

be planted in autumn, but usually they will not flower for 3 years.

Crocus chrysanthus

syn. *Crocus cannulatus* var. *chrysanthus*, *C. croceus*

This species has bright golden yellow flowers feathered with bronze, and yellow anthers; they appear in late winter or early

Crocus chrysanthus

Crocus chrysanthus 'Gipsy Girl'

Crocus gargaricus

spring. Leaves up to 10 in (25 cm) long appear at the same time as the flowers. Hybrid cultivars include: **'Cream Beauty'** (creamy yellow flowers); **'Dorothy'** (deep golden yellow flowers); **'E. A. Bowles'** (deep butter yellow flowers with bronze feathering mainly at the base of the petals); **'Gipsy Girl'** (yellow flowers, striped purplish brown on the outside); and **'Lady-killer'** (white, heavily suffused with purple on the outside). ZONES 4–9.

Crocus gargaricus

This is a rare species from western Turkey, where it grows in mountain meadows above the ancient city of Boursa. It bears golden yellow flowers in spring, and rapidly builds into clumps by underground stolons. It tolerates slightly damper conditions than some of the other Asiatic crocuses. ZONES 7–9.

Crocus tommasinianus

This dainty species from the northern Balkans grows about 4 in (10 cm) tall with lavender to purple, sometimes white-throated flowers with a very slender white tube,

Crocus chrysanthus 'Ladykiller'

Crocus tommasinianus

appearing in late winter. One of the more easily grown species, it does well in a rockery, or naturalized under deciduous trees. 'Ruby Giant' has dark purple flowers and 'Whitewell Purple' has reddish purple flowers with silver throat markings. ZONES 5–9.

Crocus vernus
Dutch crocus

This species grows to 4 in (10 cm) high and bears solitary white, pink or purple flowers from spring to early summer. The **Dutch Hybrids**

Crocus tommasinianus 'Ruby Giant'

are vigorous plants with large flowers up to 6 in (15 cm) long, in a varied color range—white to yellow, purple or bluish; there are also some striped varieties. '**Remembrance**' has violet flowers with purple bases; '**Pickwick**' has white flowers striped with pale and dark lilac, with dark purple at the base; '**Queen of the Blues**' has lilac-blue flowers; and '**Vanguard**' has pale lilac flowers with a flush of gray on the outside. It flowers in winter. ZONES 4–9.

CYCLAMEN

This genus consists of about 20 species of tuberous perennials, native to the Mediterranean region and southwest Asia. The round tubers sit on or just below the soil surface and bear fleshy, heart-shaped leaves often with light or dark patterns on the upper surface. The elegant flowers, borne singly on bare stalks, are downward-pointing, with 5 twisted petals sharply reflexed and erect. Colors vary from crimson-red to pink or white and may be scented. Many smaller species are choice rock garden plants; the larger florist's cyclamen (*Cyclamen persicum*) is grown indoors.
CULTIVATION Cyclamens vary from frost tender to very frost

Crocus vernus 'Remembrance'

Cyclamen hederifolium

hardy. Plant in light, fibrous soil, rich in organic matter, in sun or part-shade. Tubers are best left undisturbed. Propagate from seed in autumn. Some cyclamens are susceptible to black rot.

Cyclamen hederifolium
syn. *Cyclamen neapolitanum*

This species flowers in autumn and can produce corms 6 in (15 cm) wide. Growing to 4 in (10 cm), it has dark green leaves marbled in

paler green, with broad, shallow toothing. The flowers are white to rose pink, darker at the base, and some strains are perfumed. It has a wide distribution in southern Europe and Turkey. ZONES 5–10.

Cyclamen persicum

This species occurs in woodlands from Greece to Lebanon and in North Africa. Selected strains are the florist's cyclamens, commonly grown indoors. They can be quite

Cyclamen persicum

large, up to 12 in (30 cm) tall and of similar spread. From among the crowded heart-shaped leaves, which are often marbled light and dark green with silver bands, rise large waxy flowers in shades of white, pink, purple or red, sometimes ruffled or edged with a contrasting tone. It flowers profusely over a long winter season; cool nights will ensure that flowering continues. ZONES 9–10.

CYRTANTHUS

Fire lily

This genus of about 50 species is native to southern Africa. The scented, brightly colored flowers are usually tubular and curved, mostly grouped in an umbel at the top of a hollow stem and are often nodding. They bloom at various times, depending on the species. The fleshy, somewhat grass-like leaves usually die down over winter. They do well in containers and make long-lasting cut flowers. They hybridize freely, and nurseries may offer them by color rather than by their specific names.

CULTIVATION Most are somewhat frost tender and do best in areas where winters are mild. Plant in rich, well-drained soil in a sunny situation. The neck of the bulb should be at ground level; water well through the growing season. Bulbs are best left undisturbed but may need dividing if overcrowded. Propagate from bulb offsets or seed planted in spring.

Cyrtanthus elatus
syn. *Cyrtanthus purpureus, Vallota speciosa*
Scarborough lily

From South Africa's Western Cape Province, this species is different in appearance from most others in the genus, with clumps of crowded, fairly broad leaves and bright scarlet flowers opening out into broad funnels about 3 in (8 cm) wide in late summer. ZONES 9–11.

Cyrtanthus elatus

DE

DAHLIA

This genus of about 30 species from Mexico and Central America has had a big impact on gardens. Of this number only two or three species were used to create the thousands of named varieties now on the market. Progeny of *Dahlia coccinea* and *D. pinnata* originally formed the nucleus of the modern hybrid dahlias; others are derived from forms of *D. hortensis*. So many different flower forms have been developed that the hybrids are classified into about 10 different groups, determined by the size and type of their flowerheads. Some authorities suggest that there should be more, as group 10 consists of disparate classes as yet too small to give groupings of their own, known as the miscellaneous group. Most groups have small-, medium- and large-flowered subdivisions.

CULTIVATION Dahlias are not particularly frost resistant so in cold climates the tubers are usually lifted and stored in a frost-free place to be split and replanted in spring. Most prefer a sunny, sheltered position in well-fertilized, well-drained soil. Feed monthly and water well when in flower. Increase flower size by pinching out the 2 buds alongside each center bud. All, apart from bedding forms, need staking. Propagate bedding forms from seed, others from seed, cuttings from tubers or by division.

Dahlia Hybrids

The 10 main groups of dahlia hybrids are:

Single-flowered (Group 1): These hybrids have a single ring of ray petals (sometimes 2) with an open center. Most singles usually grow

---

Useful Tip

Always consider how tall a bulb grows when you plant it. If in doubt, drive in stake at planting time rather than risk damaging the bulb later.

Dahlia, Group 1, 'Yellow Hammer'

Dahlia, Group 3, cultivar

no more than 18 in (45 cm) high, so they are ideal for bedding, for example, **'Yellow Hammer'**.
Anemone-flowered (Group 2): This group includes fewer cultivars than most of the others. They have one or more rows of outer ray florets; instead of the yellow center, these tiny flowers have mutated into outward-pointing tubular florets.

Dahlia, Group 4, 'Gerrie Hoek'

Dahlia, Group 4, 'Cameo'

Dahlia, Group 5, 'Majuba'

Collarette (Group 3): Collarettes have a single row of 8 outer large florets, usually flat and rounded at the tips. Then comes a row of shorter tubular, wavy florets often in a contrasting color and finally the normally yellow center.

Waterlily or nymphaea-flowered (Group 4): Fully double-flowered with slightly cupped petals, these dahlias resemble the waterlilies. **'Cameo'** and **'Gerrie Hoek'** are popular.

Decorative (Group 5): These dahlias are fully double-flowered with no central disc showing. The petals are more numerous and slightly twisted making the flower look fuller than the waterlily types.

This group, which can produce some truly giant forms, may be subdivided into formal decoratives and informal ones. Informal decoratives have petals that are twisted or pointed and of an irregular arrangement. **'Hamari Gold'** is a giant decorative with golden bronze flowers. **'Majuba'** is a freeflowering compact, medium-sized decorative dahlia bearing deep red blooms on strong stems. Large informal decorative types include

Useful Tip

If mail order spring bulbs arrive late, plant them right away or pot them. Don't attempt to keep them dry over winter until spring.

Dahlia, Group 5, 'Golden Ballade'

'**Golden Ballade**', with deep gold flowers; '**Almand's Climax**', which has lavender flowers with paler tips; '**Alva's Supreme**', with yellow flowers; and '**Suffolk Punch**', with rich purple flowers.

Ball (Group 6): As suggested by the name, these dahlias are full doubles and almost ball shaped. Miniature, small, medium and large forms are available. '**Rose Cupid**' is a medium-sized ball dahlia and '**Wotton Cupid**' is a dark pink miniature.

Pompon (Group 7): These are similar to ball dahlias but even more globose and usually not much more than 2 in (5 cm) across. They are sometimes called "Drum Stick" dahlias. '**Buttercup**' is a pompon form. '**Small World**' has pure white blooms and reaches a height of 3 ft (1 m), with an approximate spread of 24 in (60 cm).

Cactus-flowered (Group 8): These fully double-flowered dahlias have long, narrow rolled petals, which give the flowers a spidery look. This group can be divided further by size as well as into classes with straight petals, incurved petals or recurved petals. '**Hamari Bride**' is a medium-sized white form. The **Garden Party** dahlias are particularly attractive.

Semi-cactus (Group 9): As the name suggests, this group is close to Group 8 but the petals are broader at the base and less rolled back at the edges. '**Brandaris**' is a medium form with soft orange and golden yellow flowers; '**Hayley Jane**' is a small form with purplish pink flowers and white bases; and '**Salmon Keene**' has large salmon pink to golden flowers.

Dahlia, Group 6, 'Rose Cupid'

Dahlia, Group 8, Garden Party cultivar

Miscellaneous (Group 10): This category consists of small groups and unique forms of dahlias that do not fit into any of the above groups, such as the orchid types which are single with revolute petals. The star dahlias are also single in appearance and produce very pointed, widely spaced petals. Peony-flowered dahlias, which are still kept as a separate group in some countries, commonly have one or two rows of

Dahlia, Group 9, 'Brandaris'

Dahlia, Group 10, 'Bishop of Llandaff'

flat petals with a center which can be open or partly covered by small twisted petals; examples of this form include '**Bishop of Llandaff**', with brilliant scarlet blooms above beautiful deep burgundy leaves, and '**Tally Ho**', with deep orange flowers and gray-green, purple-tinged leaves. ZONES 8–10.

Dahlia, Group 10, 'Tally Ho'

ERANTHIS

Winter aconite

From Europe and temperate Asia, the 7 species in this genus of clump-forming perennials have been grown for centuries and are valued for their ability to naturalize under deciduous trees and their habit of flowering in late winter and early spring. The short-stemmed, yellow, buttercup-like flowers are surrounded by an attractive ruff of green leaves. They mix pleasantly with other early-flowering, bulbous plants, such as daffodils.

CULTIVATION Very frost hardy, winter aconite grows in full sun or part-shade. Slightly damp conditions during the summer dormancy period and an alkaline, well-drained soil are conducive to good growth and plentiful flowers. Propagate from seed in late spring or by division of the clump in autumn.

Eranthis hyemalis
syn. *Eranthis hymalis*, Cilica Group

Indigenous to Europe, this ground-hugging perennial with knobbly tubers grows to a height of 3 in (8 cm). The yellow, cup-shaped flowers, to 1 in (25 mm) across, are borne above a ruff of lobed leaves. ZONES 5–9.

Eranthis hyemalis (foreground)

EREMURUS

Foxtail lily, desert candle

This is a genus of 50 or more species, all native to the cold, high plains of central and western Asia. Among the most dramatic of early summer perennials, they are mainly clump forming with a rosette of strap-shaped leaves. Their flower spikes, each of which can contain hundreds of flowers in pale shades of white, yellow or pink, rise to well over head height. The foliage is luxuriant but low, so the flower stems rise almost naked, making them all the more imposing.

CULTIVATION In the wild these cool- to cold-climate plants are protected from the winter cold by a thick blanket of snow; however, in milder climates, they must be given a winter mulch to ensure the soil does not freeze. The other requirements are sun, a well-drained soil and shelter from strong winds. Propagate from fresh seed in autumn or by careful division after flowering.

Eremurus aitchisonii
syn. *Eremurus elwesii*

Native to Afghanistan, this is a clump-forming perennial to 6 ft (1.8 m) tall with glossy, narrow, lance-shaped leaves to 24 in (60 cm) long and spikes of pale pink flowers in late spring to early summer. ZONES 6–9.

Eremurus aitchisonii

E. × *isabellinus* 'Shelford Desert Candle'

Eremurus × isabellinus, Shelford Hybrids

These frost-hardy perennials are grown for their lofty spikes of close-packed flowers, magnificent for floral displays. They produce rosettes of strap-like leaves and in midsummer, each crown yields spikes of bloom with strong stems and hundreds of shallow cup-shaped flowers in a wide range of colors including white, pink, salmon, yellow, apricot and coppery tones. 'Shelford Desert Candle' is a particularly lovely, pure white form. 'Cleopatra' has attractive orange flowers. ZONES 5–9.

Eremurus robustus

The tallest of the foxtail lilies, this upright perennial from central Asia flowers profusely in early summer. The individual flowers are smallish stars in palest peach-pink and are produced by the hundreds in spires that can reach nearly 10 ft (3 m) in height. They need to be staked. ZONES 6–9.

ERYTHRONIUM

Dog's tooth violet, trout lily, fawn lily

Native to temperate Eurasia and North America, these little perennial lilies bear delicate, reflexed, star-shaped flowers in spring. They come in shades of yellow or pink, and there are some very pretty hybrids available. The dark green foliage is often attractively mottled. The common name of

Eremurus robustus

dog's tooth violet refers to the odd shape of the tuber.

CULTIVATION Frost hardy, they do best in cooler areas. Plant the tubers in autumn in part-shade in well-drained, humus-rich soil, and keep moist. In the right conditions they multiply easily and should be left undisturbed until over-crowding occurs. Propagate from offsets in summer or from seed in autumn. Some species are more difficult to grow than others.

Erythronium revolutum
Pink trout lily

The leaves are mottled and the stalks are frequently, but not always, suffused with a pinkish glow. The

Erythronium tuolumnense

petal color can vary between pink, purple and white with yellow central bands and yellow anthers. It reaches about 12 in (30 cm) in height. '**Pagoda**' has marbled green foliage and nodding, deep yellow flowers; '**Pink Beauty**' is a robust form with rich pink flowers. ZONES 5–9.

Erythronium tuolumnense
Tuolumne fawn lily

This native of central California grows on the foothills of the Sierra Nevada in open pine and oak woods. The leaves are mid-green to 8 in (20 cm) long and the flowers, which appear in late spring, are small, deep yellow and star-like. It reaches 12 in (30 cm) in height. ZONES 5–9.

Erythronium revolutum

EUCOMIS

Pineapple lily

The 15 species of pineapple lily are all deciduous and native to southern Africa. They bear spikes of small, star-shaped flowers with crowning tufts of leaves much like a pineapple. They grow from enlarged bulbs, and the basal rosette of glossy foliage is both quite handsome and somewhat bulky—these are not bulbs to slip in between other plants but rather substantial border plants in their own right. The Xhosa people use the bulbs, boiled into a poultice, as a relief from rheumatism.
CULTIVATION Marginally frost hardy, these plants do best in warm-temperate climates in full sun in moist but well-drained soil; they dislike water during the dormant winter months. Where there is a danger of frost reaching the bulbs they are best grown as pot plants and wintered safely indoors. Propagate either from seed or by division of the clumps in spring.

Eucomis comosa
syn. *Eucomis punctata*

This species grows to about 30 in (75 cm) in height. Dark green, crinkly, strap-like leaves surround the tall, purple-spotted scapes. The hundreds of flowers, white to green and sometimes spotted with purple, are borne in late summer and autumn. Water well through the growing season. It makes an excellent, long-lasting cut flower. There is also a purple-leafed form—both stems and leaves are deep purple.
ZONES 8–10.

Eucomis comosa

FG

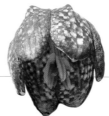

FREESIA

There are around 6 species in this genus of South African cormous perennials, admired for their bright, goblet-shaped, deliciously scented spring flowers. The wild species can have blooms of yellow, pink or purple, but the many hybrids have extended the range to most colors, as well as pure white. The narrow, sword-shaped leaves fan out at the base of the plants. They make very good cut flowers.

CULTIVATION Freesias are marginally frost hardy and grow satisfactorily in containers in a greenhouse. In warm climates, plant corms outdoors in autumn; plant in midspring in colder climates. Grow in full sun in fertile, moist but well-drained soil. Divide the clumps in autumn. In cold climates, lift the corms for winter. Propagation is either from seed in spring or offsets in autumn.

Freesia Hybrids

Over 300 hybrids have been raised and come in a wide range of brilliant colors, although the scent of some has been diminished. The showy flowers are borne on wiry, arching stems, easily flattened by rain or wind, so some form of shelter or staking is advisable. ZONES 9–10.

Freesia Hybrids

FRITILLARIA

Fritillary

There are about 100 species in this genus of bulbs, relatives of the lily and tulip, found in a variety of habitats in temperate areas of the Northern Hemisphere. Some are more easily grown than others, but the spectacle of their nodding, bell- or goblet-shaped flowers, borne mainly in spring, is worth the trouble.

CULTIVATION Mostly quite frost hardy, they do best in areas with cold winters. Plant bulbs in early autumn in part-shade in rich, organic, well-drained soil. Water well through the growing season but allow to dry out after flowering. In areas with high summer rainfall, lift bulbs gently and keep them out of the ground for as short a time as possible. Propagate from offsets in summer, but do not disturb clumps for a few years. Seed can be sown in autumn but will take 4 to 5 years to bloom.

Useful Tip

Always prepare your bulb bed to double the suggested planting depth. The roots need room to grow too, and you cannot expect the best blooms if the roots are confined and unhappy.

Fritillaria acmopetala

Fritillaria acmopetala

This species, to 15 in (38 cm) high, comes from southwestern Turkey, Cyprus, Syria and Lebanon, where plants are found in cedar forests and on limestone escarpments. The flowers have 3 green outer segments and 3 inner segments that are green stippled with brownish purple. The inside of the bell is a glowing, shiny yellow-green. The foliage is a dull gray-green. ZONES 7–9.

Fritillaria imperialis
Crown imperial

The tallest of the species, this is the easiest to grow. The leafy stems, up to 5 ft (1.5 m) high, bear whorls of lance-shaped, pale green leaves. Pendent clusters of up to 8 yellow, orange or red bell-shaped flowers appear in late spring and early summer. The flowers have an unpleasant odor. '**Lutea**' bears bright yellow flowers; '**Aureomarginata**' has variegated foliage with deep yellow margins and orange flowers; '**Prolifera**' (syn. 'Crown upon Crown') has orange-red blooms in two whorls, one above the other. ZONES 4–9.

Fritillaria meleagris
Snake's head fritillary, chequered lily

In spring, this common European species produces slender stems reaching 12 in (30 cm), each with a few slender leaves and bearing

Fritillaria imperialis 'Lutea'

one nodding, goblet-shaped bloom that is maroon, green or white, 1 in (25 mm) long, and blotched or chequered. It thrives under deciduous trees or in a rock garden, if kept moist while growing. ZONES 4–9.

GALANTHUS

Snowdrop

This genus of about 15 species of small bulbs is native to Europe and western Asia. Small, white, nodding, sometimes perfumed flowers appear above leaves like those of daffodils but much shorter. The three inner petals are

Fritillaria meleagris

Galanthus elwesii

much shorter than the outer three which usually have green markings. Snowdrops naturalize in grass or lightly shaded woodland. They also do well in a rockery and are excellent cut flowers. They flower in late winter and early spring.

Useful Tip

Bulbs most need feeding immediately after flowering. That's when they're readying their reserves for the next flowering season.

CULTIVATION Very frost hardy, they do best in cooler climates. Grow in rich, moist but well-drained soil in part-shade. In very cold areas they may be planted in full sun. Propagate from fresh ripe seed or divide clumps immediately the flowers fade, while still in leaf.

Galanthus elwesii
Giant snowdrop

This species from Turkey and the Balkans multiplies well in temperate climates and has distinctive gray-blue leaves folded one inside

Galanthus nivalis 'Flore Pleno'

the other at the base. It bears nodding white flowers, with the inner petals marked by two green spots (these spots sometimes join to form a single, V-shaped mark). They flower in late winter and spring and grow to 10 in (25 cm) tall. ZONES 6–9.

Galanthus nivalis
Common snowdrop

This most commonly grown species reaches 6 in (15 cm) tall. The erect leaves are bluish green. Each stem bears a nodding, bell-shaped, 1 in (25 mm) wide, scented flower in late winter. The outer petals are white, and the inner petals have a green marking at the tip. There are

many cultivars, including the double-flowered '**Flore Pleno**'; '**Lady Elphinstone**', with gray-green foliage and double flowers; '**Pusey Green Tip**', with double flowers marked pale green on the outside; and '**Viridapicis**', with a very long spathe that is sometimes split. The **Scharlockii Group** bears slender flowers with green markings. ZONES 4–9.

GALTONIA

This genus of 4 species of frost-hardy bulbs is native to South Africa. Summer flowering, they are closely related to *Ornithogalum* though their more bell-shaped flowers set them apart. They have semi-erect, strap-like leaves in rosettes and elegant, tall spikes of pendent, funnel-shaped flowers. **CULTIVATION** Plant in a sheltered site in full sun and fertile, well-drained soil; winter damp will rot them. They tend to die down in winter and may be lifted for replanting in spring. Propagate from fresh ripe seed in spring or by offsets in autumn or spring. Snails may be a problem.

Galtonia candicans
Berg lily, summer hyacinth

This species is up to 4 ft (1.2 m) high, with fleshy gray-green leaves

Galtonia candicans

and erect stems bearing loose spikes of up to 30 pendent bell-shaped white flowers, sometimes shaded or marked with green. They are produced for about 6 weeks from midsummer. ZONES 6–10.

GLADIOLUS

syn. *Acidanthera, Homoglossum*

This genus of about 180 species of cormous perennials has sword-shaped leaves in fan-like tufts and is native to Africa, Europe and the Middle East. Cultivated gladioli are mainly large-flowered hybrids, grown for their showy, funnel-shaped flowers. Plants vary greatly from very small and sometimes fragrant species to the spectacular florist's gladiolus. The 3 main hybrid groups are the **Grandiflorus** (or Large-flowered) **Group**, the **Primulinus Group** and the **Nanus** (or Butterfly) **Group**.

CULTIVATION Plant corms about 4 in (10 cm) deep in well-drained, sandy soil in a sunny position. In cool areas, plant in early spring; in warm areas, plant from autumn. Water plants well in summer and cut off spent flower stems. Tall stems may need staking. When picking for display, cut when the lower flowers open. Lift corms over winter in cold climates; lift large-flowered corms in all areas, especially those with high winter rainfall; store when perfectly dry. Propagate from seed or cormlets in spring.

Gladiolus × *colvillei* 'Peach Blossom'

Gladiolus × *colvillei*
Baby gladiolus

This dainty plant bears up to ten elegant, 3 in (8 cm) dark pink, yellow or white blooms on an 18 in (45 cm) spike, usually in late spring or early summer. 'The Bride' has white flowers. There is now a range of similar hybrids, all about 15 in (38 cm) tall, with similarly blotched flowers in shades of white and

Useful Tip

For a succession of bloom, stagger the planting of summer-flowering plants such as gladiolus. Start planting in late winter and continue until midsummer.

pink. 'Peach Blossom' has pale pink flowers suffused with mauve or purple. ZONES 8–10.

Gladiolus × *colvillei* 'The Bride'

Gladiolus communis subsp. *byzantinus*

Gladiolus communis

From spring to summer this vigorous species from southern Europe produces spikes of pink flowers streaked or blotched with white or red. It grows to a height of 3 ft (1 m) and has very narrow, tough leaves. *Gladiolus communis* subsp. *byzantinus* (syn. *G. byzantinus*) bears up to 15 pink to magenta flowers in late spring to early summer. ZONES 8–10.

Gladiolus, Grandiflorus Group

These very large-flowering hybrids produce long, densely packed spikes of broadly funnel-shaped flowers in summer. The sometimes ruffled flowers are arranged in alternating fashion mostly on one side of a 3–5 ft (1–1.5 m) stem. Demanding in terms of pest and disease control, as well as requiring support to keep upright, they are grown mainly for exhibition or as commercial cut flowers. 'Green Woodpecker' has medium-sized, ruffled greenish flowers with red markings at the throat; 'Red Majesty' has lightly ruffled red flowers; 'Wine & Roses' is pink with a purple throat and a frilled edge; 'White Prosperity' has creamy white flowers; and 'Praha' is a salmon pink form with a yellow throat and red center. ZONES 7–10.

G., Grandiflorus Group, 'Red Majesty'

HI

HYACINTHOIDES

syn. *Endymion*

Bluebell

The frost-hardy European blue-bells, vigorous, bulbous perennials with attractive, scented flowers, are popular with gardeners in temperate regions worldwide. They have strap- to lance-shaped, basal leaves. The flowers are usually blue or white but sometimes pink. The 3 or 4 species are equally happy in a rock garden, naturalized under deciduous trees or in flower borders.

CULTIVATION Bluebells thrive in moist, part-shaded conditions. Bulbs should be planted in rich, moist soil in autumn. Water well until the flowers start to die. They should multiply freely but are best left undisturbed for a few years, and then divided in late summer.

Hyacinthoides hispanica

syn. *Endymion hispanicus, Scilla campanulata, S. hispanica*

Spanish bluebell

The Spanish bluebell is the most popular and easily grown species in the *Hyacinthoides* genus. It grows to about 12 in (30 cm) and flowers in spring. The 1 in (25 mm) wide,

Hyacinthoides hispanica

Hyacinthoides hispanica 'Azalea'

nodding, bell-shaped flowers are lilac to blue. The bright green foliage is strap-like. It multiplies freely. '**Azalea**' is a compact, free-flowering form with many shorter spikes of pink-lilac flowers. A very similar plant, ***H. non-scripta*** (syn. *Endymion non-scriptus, Scilla non-scripta*), the English bluebell,

Hyacinthoides non-scripta (white form)

flowers from early spring to summer. The pink, white or lavender blue, fragrant flowers are about $\frac{1}{2}$ in (12 mm) long. ZONES 5–10.

HYACINTHUS

Hyacinth

There are 3 species in this genus of bulbs from Asia Minor and central Asia, all spring flowering. Bulbs are squat and have a tunic of fleshy scales. The glossy green leaves, which appear just as the flower spike is emerging, are narrow and strap-like, while the blooms are crowded onto a short spike. The individual flowers are either tubular or strongly reflexed and are sweetly and pervasively perfumed. **CULTIVATION** Plant bulbs about 4 in (10 cm) deep in autumn or at the start of winter in mild

Hyacinthoides non-scripta

climates. They do best in full sun except in climates with mild winters where some shade helps keep the bulbs cool. After flowering, the bulbs can be left in the ground, but there are far fewer flowers on the spike the following year. For a reliable display, plant fresh bulbs each year.

Hyacinthus orientalis

Popular with gardeners all over the world, the many named varieties of hyacinths are cultivars of *Hyacinthus orientalis*, which originally comes from the Middle East and Mediterranean region. The wild form has far fewer flowers and rather more leaves than the cultivated varieties. A spike of flowers is massed atop a 12 in (30 cm) stem. The spring flowers vary enormously in color, for example, '**City of Haarlem**' produces a strong spike of creamy yellow flowers late in the season; '**Columbus**' has creamy white

Hyacinthus orientalis

Hyacinthus orientalis 'Columbus'

Hyacinthus orientalis 'King of the Blues'

blossoms, long and tubular, without reflexed petals; **'Lady Derby'** has flowers in the softest pastel pink; and **'King of the Blues'**, as the name implies, is blue. Flowers are also available in purples and reds. ZONES 5–9.

HYMENOCALLIS

syn. *Ismene*
Spider lily, filmy lily

There are about 40 species of *Hymenocallis* found in a variety of habitats from the southern US to South America. Some are evergreen and all are deliciously scented. The unusual, beautiful white flowers of the spider lilies resemble daffodils except for the delicate, spider-like petals surrounding the inner corona.
CULTIVATION Most species are tropical plants and prefer a warm, frost-free climate; in colder areas they need the shelter of a greenhouse. They can also be grown as indoor pot plants. Plant bulbs in

Hyacinthus orientalis 'Lady Derby'

winter, about 6 in (15 cm) deep,
in well-drained soil. A part-shaded
position is best. Water very well
during growth and never allow to
dry out completely. Offsets form
quickly and should be divided in
winter.

Hymenocallis narcissiflora
syn. *Ismene calathina*
Basket flower, Peruvian daffodil

Hymenocallis narcissiflora is the most
widely grown species, often planted
as a summer bulb like *Gladiolus*. It
is native to the Peruvian Andes. Its
broad, white flowers are very showy,
with wide petals reflexed behind
the green-tinged cup. The flowers
appear in early summer. A pale
yellow form exists. ZONES 9–11.

Hymenocallis narcissiflora

IRIS

This genus of about 300 species,
native to a wide range of habitats
in the temperate regions of the
Northern Hemisphere, is named
for the Greek goddess of the rain-
bow. Each distinctive flower has
6 petals: 3 outer petals, called
"falls," which droop away from
the center and alternate with the
inner petals, called "standards."
There are many hybrids. Irises
are divided into 2 main groups:
rhizomatous and bulbous.
Rhizomatous irises have sword-

shaped leaves, are sometimes evergreen, and are subdivided into 3
groups: **bearded** (or flag) irises,
with a tuft of hairs (the "beard")
on the 3 lower petals; **beardless**
irises, without the tuft; and
crested or **Evansia** irises, with
a raised crest instead of a beard.

The bulbous irises are also
divided into 3 groups: the **Juno,
Reticulata** and **Xiphium** irises.
The first 2 consist of beautiful,
but mostly difficult bulbs, from
west and central Asia. However,
the Xiphium irises are easier to
grow; they have given rise to a
group of bulbous hybrids including the so-called **English, Spanish**
and **Dutch** irises. The latter are
the popular florist's flowers.
CULTIVATION Growing conditions vary greatly. Rhizomatous
irises, with the exception of the
crested or Evansia irises, are frost
hardy and prefer a sunny position;
some beardless types like very

Iris ensata

moist soil. Bulbous irises prefer a sunny position with ample moisture during growth, but very little during their summer dormant period. Plant bulbous irises in autumn, and keep free of aphids. Propagate by division in late summer after flowering or from seed in autumn. Named cultivars should only be divided.

Iris ensata
syn. *Iris kaempferi*
Japanese flag, higo iris

Native to Japan, this beardless iris grows to 3 ft (1 m) tall. It bears purple flowers from late spring to early summer, with yellow blotches on each fall. The leaves have a prominent midrib. The many named cultivars bear huge flowers, up to 10 in (25 cm) wide, in shades of white, lavender, blue and purple, often blending 2 shades, and some

Iris ensata 'Exception'

with double flowers. They prefer part-shade in hot areas, rich, acid soil and plenty of moisture. They can even grow in shallow water, provided they are not submerged during the winter months. The foliage dies down in winter. 'Exception' has particularly large falls and deep purple flowers; 'Mystic Buddha' has purple-blue flowers with red edging. 'Moonlight Waves' has white flowers with lime green centers. ZONES 4–10.

Iris missouriensis

syn. *Iris tolmeiana*

Missouri flag, Rocky Mountain iris

A widespread rhizomatous, beardless iris extending through western and central North America from Mexico to British Columbia, this is a very frost-hardy and easy-to-grow plant. It reaches 30 in (75 cm) in height. It likes moist soil up until it flowers in early spring and drier conditions during summer. This species can make substantial clumps. Its flowers vary in color from very pale blue through to deep blue or lavender, with some white forms. The falls, veined with deep purple, usually have a yellow blaze. ZONES 3–9.

Iris pallida

Dalmatian iris

This bearded iris from the Dalmatian region of Croatia has pale blue, fragrant flowers with yellow beards, borne on 4 ft (1.2 m) high stems in late spring. It is often grown as a source of orris (also

Iris missouriensis

Iris pallida 'Variegata'

obtained from *Iris germanica* 'Florentina'), a volatile substance that develops in the dried and aged rhizomes and is used in perfumes, dental preparations and breath fresheners. **'Variegata'** (syn. 'Aurea Variegata') has handsome leaves, striped gray-green and cream. ZONES 5–10.

Iris reticulata
Netted iris, reticulated iris

This bulbous Reticulata iris grows to 4 in (10 cm) high when it is in flower. Several named varieties are available, differing mainly in the shade of blue of the showy flowers. The foliage is short during the late winter to early spring-flowering time, becoming longer after bloom.

The leaves are quadrangular in cross-section and although these are often scarcely visible at flowering, some forms will have leaves taller than the flowers. It prefers sun and perfectly drained soil; it is very frost hardy and does best in cold winter climates. The flowers are scented and it makes a delightful pot plant. Some of its hybrids and forms (often crossed with *Iris histrioides*) include **'Gordon'**, with light blue flowers with an orange blotch on a white background, and **'Joyce'**, a lavender-blue standard with sky-blue falls marked gray-brown and yellow. ZONES 3–10.

Iris sibirica
Siberian flag

This is one of the most popular beardless irises, usually found in

Iris reticulata 'Gordon'

Iris reticulata 'Joyce'

gardens as one of its cultivars rather than in its wild form. The plants make strongly vertical clumps of slender, bright green leaves 2–4 ft (0.6–1.2 m) high. In late spring or early summer, flowering stems rise above the foliage with narrow-petaled, blue, purple or white flowers, often veined in a deeper color. It prefers full sun to very light shade (particularly in hot areas), and a moderately moist, rich soil that may be slightly acid. Water during the hottest periods. It will grow in a wet soil and does best in cold winter climates. Cultivars include '**Perry's Blue**', which has rich lilac-blue flowers with yellow markings and netted brown toward the base of the falls; '**Ruby**', which has purplish blue flowers; and

'**White Swirl**', which has pure white flowers with yellow at the base and flared, rounded petals. ZONES 4–9.

Iris sibirica 'Ruby'

Iris, Tall Bearded, 'Blue Shimmer'

Iris, **Bearded Hybrids**

Often classed under *Iris germanica* or *I. pallida*, which are only 2 of their ancestral species, the bearded irises are among the most widely grown of late-spring flowers, with fat creeping rhizomes, handsome sword-shaped, grayish foliage and stems bearing several large flowers. They are available in an enormous range of colors—everything but true red —with many varieties featuring blended colors, contrasting standards and falls, or a broad band of color around basically white flowers—this pattern is called "plicata." Some of the newer varieties, described as "remontant,"

flower a second time in late summer or autumn, though rather erratically. All prefer a temperate climate, sun and mildly alkaline, well-drained soil, and flower most freely if not over-watered in summer. Bearded irises are subdivided into 3 groups: **Dwarf Bearded**, which grow 6–15 in (15–40 cm) tall and flower earlier than the others. **Intermediate Bearded**, about 24 in (60 cm) tall, which flower a fortnight or so later than the dwarf varieties. '**Sunny Dawn**' is typical, with yellow flowers with red beards. **Tall Bearded** irises are the last to bloom and grow to 3 ft (1 m) tall or slightly higher. Representative Tall Bearded cultivars include '**Almaden**', with standards and falls in a rich burgundy; '**Beyond**', with

Iris, Tall Bearded, 'Dancer's Veil'

a creamy apricot background and red-brown plicata edging; '**Blue Shimmer**' has white flowers with lilac-blue stitching; '**Dancer's Veil**', to 3 ft (1 m) tall, has white flowers with plicata edges in blue-violet;

'**Jelly Roll**' has pink flowers with a red beard; '**Light Beam**' has yellow standards and white falls edged with yellow; and '**Orange Celebrity**' is renowned for its ideal form and brilliant yet delicate colors, including

Iris, Tall Bearded, 'Orange Celebrity'

Iris, Tall Bearded, 'Supreme Sultan'

apricot and pink shades with a flaming orange beard. '**Stepping Out**' produces 8 to 11 white flowers with purple plicata edges on each stem; it reaches 3 ft (1 m) in height and bears flowers in mid-spring. '**Blue-eyed Brunette**' has coppery brown standards and falls, with a blue spot on each fall. '**Cannington Skies**' has mid-blue standards and falls. '**Early Light**' has lemon-flushed cream standards, with slightly darker falls, and yellow

beards. '**Supreme Sultan**' has butterscotch-yellow standards and crimson-brown falls. ZONES 5–10.

Iris, Dutch Hybrids

From the Xiphium group, these bulbous irises derive their purity of color from the northern African *Iris tingitana*; their other main parent, *I. xiphium*, tends toward purple. They prefer sun and well-drained, slightly alkaline soil, but will also grow in acidic soil. Ranging in color from pale blue to almost violet, hybrids include '**Blue Magic**', with flowers in the middle of the color range, and the purplish blue '**Professor Blaauw**', one of the most widely grown flower shop irises in the world and named for Professor A. H. Blaauw (1882–1942), whose pioneering studies led to the modern techniques of inducing irises to bloom every season of the year. ZONES 7–10.

Iris, Dutch Hybrid, 'Professor Blaauw'

LM

LEUCOJUM

Snowflake

This genus consists of 10 species of bulbous perennials, resembling the snowdrop, which bear delightful flowers that bloom in spring and autumn. They are native to North Africa and the southern Mediterranean. The pendent, bell-shaped flowers consist of 6 petals, borne singly or in twos and threes at the top of a thin stem growing up to 24 in (60 cm). The mid-green to deep green leaves are narrow and strap-like. The bulbs multiply freely, and large clumps of nodding blooms make a glorious display.

CULTIVATION Some of the species prefer part-shade in moist soil, while others thrive in sunny positions with well-drained soil; they are moderately to fully frost hardy. Plant bulbs in late summer or early autumn and only lift for dividing when they produce few flowers and many leaves. Propagate from offsets in spring or early autumn or from seed sown in autumn.

Leucojum aestivum
Summer snowflake, giant snowflake

This dainty, frost hardy, spring-flowering bulb is native to Europe and western Asia. The fragrant flowers are white with a green spot near the tip of each petal and are borne in clusters atop 18 in (45 cm) stems. The blue-green leaves are long and slender. *Leucojum aestivum* var. *pulchellum* is found in the wild

Leucojum aestivum var. *pulchellum*

near or in water. Growing to a height of 24 in (60 cm), it naturalizes freely in similar situations and climates and grows in sun or shade. The flowers, 3 to 6 per stalk, carry 6 white, green-spotted petals of equal length and appear in late spring and early summer. The strap-shaped leaves, which are poisonous to stock, form voluminous clumps. 'Gravetye' is a robust form that prefers moisture-retentive soils. ZONES 4–10.

Leucojum vernum
Spring snowflake

A native of central Europe that blooms in late winter and early spring, this species grows to a height of 18 in (45 cm). Spring snowflake naturalizes freely in damp conditions, in sun or shade, and survives dry summers in style. The leaves are strap-like and the bell-shaped flowers, 2 to a stalk, carry white petals of equal length that are marked with either a green or a yellow spot. *Leucojum vernum* var. *carpathicum* has one or two flowers per stem, each with yellow-tipped petals. ZONES 5–10.

LILIUM

Lily, lilium

Many plants are referred to as "lilies," usually signifying that they belong to the lily family or one of its allied families, but in the narrowest sense this word means a member of the bulbous genus *Lilium*; this consists of around 100 species, native in temperate Eurasia (extending to high mountains of the Philippines) and North America, with the largest number found in China and the Himalayas. All species grow from buried bulbs consisting of overlapping fleshy scales, which

Lilium martagon

Lilium hybrid (Turk's cap type)

do not encircle one another as in the classical onion-type bulb. The stems are elongated with spirally arranged or whorled leaves that vary from narrow and grass-like to very short and broad. One to many 6-petaled flowers are borne in terminal sprays, the blooms erect, nodding or pendent and often with strongly recurved petals—the so-called "Turk's cap" type. Lilies vary in their growth habit, their method of reproduction and the shape, size and color of their flowers. Most of them flower in summer.

CULTIVATION Lilium bulbs, unlike those of many other genera, have no outer protective coat so should be out of the ground for the shortest possible time. The most important requirement of lilies is good drainage. Almost all like sun but a cool root area, which means they should be planted quite deeply: a minimum of 4 in (10 cm) of soil over the bulb. Most can be left undisturbed for many years and allowed to multiply naturally. Propagate from offsets from the main bulb, from bulb scales or seed or, in some species, from bulbils which form in the leaf axils up the stem.

Lilium martagon
Common Turk's cap lily

This species grows to 6 ft (1.8 m) and can produce as many as 50 blooms. The flowers are pendulous

Lilium regale

and generally creamy white to pale purple with darker spots, although many forms exist, some with deep burgundy or mahogany red flowers. It is fully frost hardy and will grow in sun or shade. ***Lilium martagon*** var. ***album*** bears pure white flowers. ZONES 4–10.

Lilium regale
Regal lily, Christmas lily

This species from western China is one of the best of the trumpet-flowered species. Growing to 6 ft (1.8 m) in height, it bears up to 30 blooms. The heavily scented flowers are white on the inside with a yellow base, flushed with carmine on the outside; each is about 6 in (15 cm) long and they are normally crowded together. The leaves are dark green and lanceolate. This species is stem rooting and produces a number of stem bulblets. 'Alum' bears pure white flowers with yellow anthers. ZONES 5–10.

Lilium, Asiatic Hybrids

Asiatic Hybrids have been bred from various central and west Asian species and form by far the largest hybrid group. They include

Lilium, Asiatic Hybrid

Lilium, Asiatic Hybrid, 'Connecticut King'

Lilium, Asiatic Hybrid, 'Roma'

most of the varieties grown commercially as cut flowers or potted plants, as well as the widely grown Mid-Century hybrids. Most, however, lack fragrance. The group has been divided into 3 subgroups: **Upward-facing:** This group is of upright habit to 30 in (75 cm) and normally flowers in early summer. '**Connecticut King**' is a popular variety with bright yellow flowers, 8 in (20 cm) in diameter; '**Enchantment**', one of the best known of all lily hybrids, bears up to 20 nasturtium-red flowers spotted with deep maroon, 6–8 in (15–20 cm) in diameter; '**Roma**' has creamy white flowers, lightly spotted and with lemon nectary channels and a ring of spots in the center of the flower; and '**Sterling Star**' is compact with white flowers up to 6 in (15 cm) across, spotted brown—it was one of the first white-flowered hybrids in the upward-facing group.

Lilium, Asiatic Hybrid, 'Sterling Star'

Outward-facing: This group is also early flowering and with an upright habit. Examples include 'Connecticut Lemon Glow', a popular cut-flower variety with bright yellow unspotted flowers and quite short stems, usually growing only 18 in (45 cm) in height.

Downward-facing: Normally a little later to flower than the others, this group includes 'Citronella', a strain rather than a single variety, with flowers ranging from pale lemon to yellow, spotted with purple-black and slightly recurving petals—there will normally be a large number of flowers on one stem; and 'Rosemary North', with dull buff-orange flowers, more or less pendulous with recurving petals and usually scented, which is unusual among the Asiatics. ZONES 5–10.

Lilium, Oriental Hybrids

Not to be confused with the so-called Asiatic hybrids, these are hybrids bred from East Asian

Lilium, Oriental Hybrid, 'Stargazer'

species such as *Lilium auratum*, *L. speciosum* and *L. japonicum* and include hybrids between these and *L. henryi*. Collectively they comprise the most spectacular of all lily hybrids. They are late flowering and may carry several flowerheads on one stem, which is inclined to make them top heavy and in need of support. All are intolerant of lime. There are 4 subgroups: trumpet-shaped flowers, bowl-shaped flowers, flat-faced flowers and recurved flowers (rarely grown). 'Imperial Silver', flat-faced with shining white flowers occasionally spotted crimson. 'Stargazer', upward-facing with bowl-shaped flowers of rich crimson with darker spots, and paler on the

Lilium, Oriental Hybrid, 'Imperial Silver'

Lilium, Oriental Hybrid, 'Yasuko'

margins of the petals. **'Yasuko'**, flat-faced flowers which are up to 10 in (25 cm) in diameter with a fine fragrance. **'Esperanto'**, bowl-shaped mid-pink flowers with a yellow mid-rib and orange spots. **'Shooting Star'** is a variety with sturdy stems and recurved cerise flowers. ZONES 6–10.

Lilium, Oriental Hybrid, 'Esperanto'

LYCORIS

Golden spider lily, resurrection lily

There are 10 to 12 species of East Asian amaryllids with spider-like flowers. The name comes from Roman history—Lycoris, famed for her beauty, was a mistress of Marc Antony. The strap-like foliage of these bulbs dies back during summer, reappearing after they bloom in summer or early autumn. Each stem carries an umbel of trumpet-shaped flowers with narrow, strongly recurved petals that usually have wavy margins, and the long stamens and styles give a spidery appearance. CULTIVATION Plant bulbs in a sunny position in rich, well-drained soil. Water during their winter growing season but they need warm, dry conditions when dormant. Moderately frost hardy, they need protection from cold winds. Clumps are best left undisturbed for a few years; they can then be divided when dormant in summer. They may also be propagated from seed.

Lycoris radiata
Red spider lily

Native to China and Japan, the red spider lily is the most commonly grown species. It has 12–18 in (30–45 cm) stems and bears, in late summer or early autumn, clusters

Lycoris radiata

of 4 or 5 rose red, 12–18 in (5–8 cm) wide flowers with strongly curled petals and long, slightly upward-curving stamens. ZONES 7–10.

MIRABILIS

Umbrella wort

This Central and South American genus consists of about 50 species of annuals or herbaceous perennials that make showy garden plants in virtually frost-free climates. Some can become invasive and difficult to eradicate as they can be quite deep rooted. The flowers are often brightly colored and, in one case at least, are variegated in bold colors like magenta and orange. Most have a pleasant fragrance.

CULTIVATION In frost-free and dry tropical climates, they are quite easy plants to grow. All that is required is a sunny, well-drained aspect. In colder climates, the tubers of perennial species can be lifted and stored over winter like dahlias. Propagate from seed or by division of the tubers.

Mirabilis jalapa

Marvel of Peru, four-o'clock flower

This bushy, tuberous perennial, native to tropical America, has

Mirabilis jalapa

fragrant, trumpet-shaped, crimson, pink, white or yellow flowers that open in late afternoon and remain open all night, closing again at dawn. It is good as a pot or bedding plant or as a dwarf hedge. It is summer flowering and grows to around 3 ft (1 m) high with a spread of 24–30 in (60–75 cm). ZONES 8–11.

MUSCARI

Grape hyacinth

The 30 or so species of this genus are natives of the Mediterranean region and western Asia. The slender, strap-like leaves are produced soon after planting, as the summer dormancy period is very short. Spikes 4 in (10 cm) long bear grape-like clusters of bright blue, pale blue, pale yellow or white flowers in early spring. CULTIVATION Frost hardy, they prefer cool areas. They look best in clumps and need rich, well-drained soil. Plant the bulbs in autumn in a sunny or part-shaded position, but protect from hot sun in warm areas. The rapidly multiplying clumps should spread freely and are best left undisturbed for a few years. Divide overcrowded bulbs or grow from seed.

Muscari botryoides

This species from central and south-eastern Europe is one of several

Muscari botryoides

species that could be defined as a classical grape hyacinth. It grows to about 8 in (20 cm) tall with semi-erect, channeled, mid-green leaves and spherical bright blue flowers with a white constricted mouth. 'Album' bears racemes of scented white flowers. ZONES 3–10.

Muscari neglectum
syn. *Muscari racemosum*
Common grape hyacinth

This is a variable species native to Europe, North Africa and south-western Asia. The tiny, urn-shaped flowers are deep blue to blue-black with a white mouth. The bright green leaves can be erect or spreading, and are sometimes stained red at soil level. ZONES 4–10.

Muscari botryoides 'Album'

Muscari neglectum

N

NARCISSUS

Daffodil, narcissus

Members of this well-known genus of bulbs from Europe, Asia and North Africa are easy to grow, multiply freely and bloom year after year. The wild species number about 50 and are mostly native to the western Mediterranean region. Many thousands of cultivars have been named, and horticultural authorities have grouped these into 12 divisions or classes, it is the first 4 which are the most important: Trumpet narcissi (Division 1), which have trumpets as long as the outer petals or perianth; the Large-cupped narcissi (Division 2), with trumpets from one-third to two-thirds as long; the Small-cupped narcissi (Division 3), with trumpets less than one-third the length of the petals; and the Double-flowered narcissi (Division 4) with double flowers, either one or several per stem. Divisions 5 to 9 cover hybrids and cultivars of important species such as *Narcissus triandrus*, *N. cyclamineus*, *N. jonquilla*, *N. tazetta* and *N. poeticus*

respectively; Division 10 covers the wild species; Division 11 the split-corona hybrids; and Division 12 consists of daffodils not included in any other division, such as *N. bulbocodium* hybrids. Flower colors range from white to yellow, although individual varieties may have white, yellow, red, orange or pink trumpets.

CULTIVATION Frost hardiness of these bulbs varies, but all tolerate at least light frosts. Plant in

Narcissus, Div. 1, (Trumpet daffodils)

Narcissus, Div. 1, 'Chivalry'

Narcissus, Div. 1, 'Las Vegas'

autumn, 4–6 in (10–15 cm) deep in rich, well-drained soil. They enjoy full sun in cool areas, and some shade in warmer areas. Feed the bulbs after flowering. Clumps will multiply freely and should be left undisturbed for a few years; thereafter lift and divide in autumn.

Narcissus, Trumpet daffodils (Division 1)

These are the best known of all the daffodils, with their solitary large flowers and long trumpets. They are derived mainly from the wild daffodil *Narcissus pseudonarcissus*. There are innumerable named cultivars, which may be all yellow; white with yellow trumpets; all white; or white with pale pink trumpets. They are the first of the big daffodils to flower. '**King Alfred**', raised in 1890, is the classic cultivar, but its name has been very loosely applied. '**Arctic**

Gold', '**Chivalry**', '**Las Vegas**' and '**Dutch Master**' are among the most popular. ZONES 4–10.

Narcissus, Large-cupped daffodils (Division 2)

Flowering a week or two later than the trumpets, this is a large division with many named varieties. They originate mainly from the cross *Narcissus poeticus* × *pseudonarcissus* (or *N.* × *incomparabilis*). The popular pink-cupped cultivars with their white perianths mostly belong here, but there are many others in various

Narcissus, Div. 2, 'Ambergate'

Narcissus, Div. 2, 'Fortune'

Narcissus, Div. 3, 'Amore'

combinations of white or yellow perianths with cups in white, yellow, orange or red. '**Exotic Pink**' and '**Passionale**' are pink-cupped daffodils, while '**Ambergate**' and '**Fortune**' have brilliant orange coronas. Both the perianth and the corona of '**Ice Follies**' are white. '**Bantam**' is another popular cultivar. ZONES 4–10.

Narcissus, Small-cupped daffodils (Division 3)

Of similar origin to Division 2, these resemble the Trumpet and

Large-cupped daffodils except for their smaller cups. Like them, they come in many named cultivars. They flower at the same time as the Large-cupped types. '**Merlin**' has flowers with pure white perianths and pale yellow cups; '**Amore**' has a white perianth and a primrose cup that fades to orange at the rim; '**St. Keverne**' has a white perianth and cup; and '**Whitbourne**' is another lovely daffodil in this group. ZONES 4–10.

Narcissus, Div. 2, 'Bantam'

Narcissus, Div. 3, 'Whitbourne'

Narcissus, Div. 4, 'Acropolis'

Narcissus, Div. 4, 'Unique'

Narcissus, Double-flowered daffodils (Division 4)

These daffodils can have either a solitary large flower or several smaller ones, with the perianth segments or the corona, or both, doubled. The double-flowered daffodils are less popular than many other types because they tend to be late flowering and their buds will not open properly if they have undergone dry conditions while developing. '**Acropolis**', '**Tahiti**' and '**Unique**' are among the most popular. ZONES 4–10.

Narcissus, Div. 4, 'Tahiti'

Narcissus, Triandrus daffodils (Division 5)

The type species *Narcissus triandrus* is native to Spain; it is rarely cultivated, but this division includes garden forms of the species. All have pendent, nodding flowers, a straight-edged cup and slightly reflexed petals. There are usually several blooms per stem. The forms vary in height from 6 to 18 in (15 to 45 cm). '**Hawera**' has yellow flowers; '**Thalia**' has pale yellow petals and a white cup with 3 or more blooms per stem. ZONES 4–9.

Narcissus, Cyclamineus daffodils (Division 6)

These hybrids bear the characteristics of *Narcissus cyclamineus* and grow to 15 in (38 cm) high. Their trumpet-shaped cups are longer than those of *N. triandrus*, and their petals are narrow and strongly reflexed. They flower in early to midspring. Popular hybrids are

Narcissus, Div. 7, 'Suzy'

'**February Gold**', an early bloomer that naturalizes well and has single, lasting flowers with yellow petals and slightly darker yellow trumpets; '**Dove Wings**', with small flowers comprising white petals and a long, primrose-yellow trumpet; and '**Tête-à-Tête**', a profuse and early flowerer with lasting blooms consisting of golden-yellow petals and an orange, frilled corona. '**Charity May**' has long-lasting, vivid, pure yellow flowers. ZONES 6–9.

Narcissus, Jonquilla daffodils (Division 7)

Possessing the characteristics of the wild jonquil of southern Europe and northern Africa, *Narcissus jonquilla*, these narcissi are scented, with cups shorter than the flat petals. There are often 2 or more blooms on a stem, which grows to 15 in (38 cm). '**Suzy**' flowers in midspring; it has golden petals and a deep orange cup. '**Stratosphere**' has 3 blooms with a cup of a deeper golden yellow than its petals. '**Trevithian**' flowers early in spring and produces up to 3 large, rounded, primrose-yellow blooms. The flowers of '**Sweetness**' are rich gold with pointed petals. ZONES 4–9.

Narcissus, Tazetta daffodils (Division 8)

These sweetly scented narcissi flower from autumn to spring and have many-flowered stems; they grow up to 15 in (38 cm). The cup is small and straight-sided, with broad, often frilled petals. This class can be further subdivided into those similar to *Narcissus tazetta* and those resulting from a cross between *N. tazetta* and *N. poeticus* and referred to as *poetaz narcissi*. '**Avalanche**' bears 15 white flowers with soft yellow cups on a single stem. '**Erlicheer**', a double, cluster-flowered daffodil, has flowers as perfect (and nearly as sweetly scented) as gardenias. '**Geranium**'

Narcissus, Div. 8, 'Erlicheer'

Narcissus, Div. 8, 'Geranium'

Narcissus, Div. 8, 'Soleil d'Or'

has a rich orange cup in a soft white perianth. **'Silver Chimes'** has creamy white flowers. **'Minnow'** has lemon-yellow cups and lighter yellow petals. **'Soleil d'Or'** is another beautiful cultivar.

Narcissus, Poeticus daffodils (Division 9)

This is a late spring- to early summer-flowering division showing the features of *Narcissus poeticus* from southern Europe. The plants grow to 18 in (45 cm) and produce one, sometimes two, blooms per

stem. The petals are white and the small cup often has a frilled red or orange rim. **'Actaea'** produces fragrant flowers in late spring, the flat, yellow cup rimmed with orange. 'Cantabile' is a popular white form. ZONES 4–9.

Narcissus, Wild species and variants (Division 10)

Horticultural societies have decreed that all the wild *Narcissus* species be grouped under this division.

Narcissus, Div. 8, 'Silver Chimes'

Narcissus, Div. 9, 'Cantabile'

Narcissus bulbocodium

Narcissus × odorus is an old hybrid with large, 2 in (5cm) wide bright yellow, fragrant flowers. '**Rugulosus**' is a more robust form with up to 4 flowers per stem. *N. **bulbocodium*** is widespread in the western Mediterranean; it grows to 6 in (15 cm) and has bright yellow flowers, with a long trumpet and sharply reflexed and insignificant petals. *N. **papyraceus*** is often regarded as a cultivar of the Tazetta daffodil

group, however, it is now known to occur wild in the western Mediterranean. Growing to 15 in (38 cm), the white, fragrant flowers have pointed petals, the corona is frilled and the stamens are orange-yellow. It flowers in late winter to spring and is an attractive indoor display grown in a bowl of gravel; in China it is grown in pots to celebrate the new year. ZONES 6–10.

Narcissus, Split-corona daffodils (Division 11)

Characterized by having coronas or cups that are split along at least a third of their length, these narcissi are also referred to as Collar, Papillon, Orchid or Split-cupped daffodils. The edges of the split coronas bend back toward the petals, and are sometimes frilled. They all flower in spring. Some of the better known include '**Baccarat**', '**Ahoy**', '**Palmares**', '**Orangery**' and '**Tiri Tomba**'. ZONES 4–10.

Narcissus papyraceus

Narcissus, Div. 11, 'Palmares'

NERINE

Guernsey lily

About 30 species of *Nerine* are grown for their heads of pretty, narrow-petaled, trumpet-shaped flowers in pink, red or white. From southern Africa, they bloom in autumn, usually before their leaves appear. Some are evergreen; others die down in summer. They can reach up to 24 in (60 cm) in height and 12 in (30 cm) in width. Species vary in the wild and readily interbreed in gardens, so not all can be easily identified. They are good plants for pots, and can be brought inside when in flower.

CULTIVATION Plant the bulbs in well-drained, sandy soil in a sunny position. They are not suitable for areas with high summer rainfall or very severe frosts. Propagate from seed or offsets in autumn; plants do not like being disturbed and may take a couple of years to flower.

Nerine bowdenii

Pink spider lily, large pink nerine

This species has a sturdy stem up to 24 in (60 cm) that bears as many as 12 pink blooms. The flowers have split, reflexed petals with a crimson rib running along their center and frilled edges. There is also a white form. '**Mark Fenwick**' (syn. 'Fenwick's Variety') has pink flowers held on dark stalks. ZONES 8–11.

Nerine flexuosa

syn. *Nerine pulchella*

On this species, a sturdy stem up to 24 in (60 cm) bears a cluster of up to 15 pink flowers with narrow, reflexed petals that have a deeper pink mid-vein. The foliage is narrow and strap-like and appears before the flowers. '**Alba**' is a white form. ZONES 8–10.

Nerine bowdenii

Nerine flexuosa 'Alba'

PRS

PARADISEA

St. Bruno's lily, paradise lily

This genus consists of 2 species of rhizomatous perennials from the mountains of southern Europe. They form small clumps of grassy to strap-like, bright green leaves and from late spring produce erect stems topped with heads of 6-petaled, funnel- to bell-shaped, white flowers up to $1\frac{1}{2}$ in (35 mm) long. The flower stems grow 1–5 ft (0.3–1.5 m) tall, depending on the species, and carry 4 to 25 blooms. **CULTIVATION** Both species will tolerate moderate frosts and prefer to be grown in moist, humus-rich soil in full sun. They must not dry out in summer. Propagate from seed or by dividing well-established clumps.

Paradisea liliastrum

In early summer, this species bears racemes of 4 to 10, 1–2 in (2.5–5 cm) long, scented, white, funnel-shaped flowers blooming on wiry, 12–24 in (30–60 cm) stems. The strappy, grayish green leaves are arranged in a basal rosette. It is a

beautiful plant but not always amenable to cultivation. ZONES 7–9.

PUSCHKINIA

Striped squill, Lebanon squill

This is a genus containing a single species, a strappy-leafed bulb native to the Caucasus, Turkey, northern Iran, northern Iraq and Lebanon. Resembling a small hyacinth or *Scilla*, it has flower stems up to 8 in (20 cm) tall. The flowers are pale blue with darker stripes, tubular, and about $\frac{1}{2}$ in (12 mm) long. **CULTIVATION** A tough little bulb well suited to rockeries or pots, it prefers a climate with a distinct winter and a cool summer.

Useful Tip

If rodents attack your bulbs, plant them in a wire-mesh cage. Try a buried cover of chicken wire to stop burrowing pests.

Grow in full sun in well-drained soil. It naturalizes well in a suitable climate. Propagate from seed or by dividing well-established clumps.

Puschkinia scilloides
syn. *Puschkinia libanotica, P. sicula*

This spring-flowering bulb has 2 semi-erect, mid-green, basal, strap-like leaves and a slim spike of up to 6 pale blue, star-shaped flowers with a darker line down the petals. The small flowers have a strong scent. ZONES 5–9.

RANUNCULUS

Buttercup

This genus of some 400 annuals and perennials is distributed throughout temperate regions worldwide. They are grown for their colorful flowers, which are bowl- or cup-shaped, 5-petaled and yellow, white, red, orange or pink. The name derives from the Latin for "frog," due to the tendency of some species to grow in bogs or shallow water. Two species of buttercups are popular folk cures for arthritis, sciatica, rheumatism and skin conditions, including the removal of warts.

CULTIVATION Most species of *Ranunculus* are easy to grow and thrive in well-drained soil, cool, moist conditions and sunny or shady locations. They are mostly fully frost hardy. Propagate from fresh seed or by division in spring or autumn. Water well through the growing season and allow to

Ranunculus asiaticus

Ranunculus asiaticus

R. asiaticus, Bloomingdale Hybrid

dry out after flowering. Keep an eye out for powdery mildew.

Ranunculus asiaticus

Persian buttercup

This frost-hardy perennial from the Mediterranean region is parent to many hybrids and cultivars. Masses of single or double flowers are borne on 15 in (38 cm) stems in spring, in many colors including yellow, orange, red, pink and white. The

Bloomingdale Hybrids are an 8 in (20 cm) strain bred specially for growing in pots. ZONES 9–10.

R. asiaticus, Bloomingdale Hybrid

Ranunculus asiaticus

R. asiaticus, Bloomingdale Hybrid

Ranunculus ficaria

Ranunculus ficaria
Lesser celandine, pilewort

From southwestern Asia, Europe and northwestern Africa, this perennial has single, almost cup-shaped, bright yellow flowers that appear in spring. It reaches only 2 in (5 cm) in height, and has glossy green leaves with silver or gold markings; the leaves die down after the flowers appear. 'Albus' has single, creamy white flowers with glossy petals. 'Brazen Hussy' has deep bronze-green leaves and shiny, deep golden yellow flowers with bronze undersides. ZONES 5–10.

RHODOHYPOXIS

Rose grass

Four to six species of these small, colorful, tuberous-rooted, perennials from high in the Drakensberg Mountains of South Africa belong in this genus, but only one species, *Rhodohypoxis baurii*, has become common in gardens. Named varieties are available, but sowing seeds from any of them will give quite a range of colors. They have grass- to strap-like, hairy leaves and produce white, pink, red or purple flowers on short stalks over long periods in summer.
CULTIVATION These plants grow well in temperate climates; in cold areas it is best to grow them in pots, a bulb frame or raised beds that can be covered in winter. They prefer full sun and well-drained, fertile, humus-rich soil that is moisture-retentive in summer and not excessively wet in winter. Propagate from seed in spring or by division in autumn.

Rhodohypoxis baurii

This alpine plant grows 3 in (8 cm) tall, each tuber producing grassy, lightly hairy leaves and, in spring, several starry flowers, 3 in (8 cm)

Rhodohypoxis baurii

wide. Colors range from pure white to various shades of pink and dark red. The central 3 petals close over the heart of the flower to protect it from the weather, and spring open when a pollinating insect alights. It soon forms a dense clump. ZONES 8–10.

ROSCOEA

These 18 species of tuberous perennials from China and the Himalayas are related to ginger *(Zingiber)*, but in appearance are more reminiscent of irises. They are grown for their orchid-like flowers, which have hooded upper petals, wide-lobed lower lips and 2 narrower petals. The leaves are lance-shaped and erect. They are most suitable for open borders and rock and woodland gardens. CULTIVATION They prefer part-

Useful Tip

Interplant with low-growing perennials such as forget-me-nots and primroses to hide the drying foliage of spring bulbs after blooming.

shade and cool, fertile, humus-rich soil that should be kept moist but well drained in summer. Provide a top-dressing of leafmold or well-rotted compost in winter, when the plants die down. Propagate from seed or by division.

Roscoea cautleoides

Bearing its yellow or orange flowers in summer, this frost-hardy species from China grows to 10 in (25 cm) tall with a 6 in (15 cm) spread. The glossy leaves are lance-shaped and erect and wrap into a hollow stem-like structure at their base. ZONES 6–9.

SCHIZOSTYLIS

A single species of grassy-leafed, rhizomatous perennial makes up this genus. It is widely distributed in South Africa where it grows beside streams. The long-flowering stems terminate in clusters of bowl-shaped, 6-petaled flowers in deep scarlet and pink; crimson flag is an excellent cut flower.

Roscoea cautleoides

Schizostylis coccinea 'Mrs. Hegarty'

CULTIVATION Frost hardy, it prefers full sun and fertile, moist soil with shelter from the cold in cool-temperate climates. Divide every couple of years when it becomes crowded, or propagate from seed in spring.

Schizostylis coccinea 'Grandiflora'

Schizostylis coccinea
Crimson flag

This variable species can fail in prolonged dry conditions. The sword-shaped leaves are green and are untidy unless pruned regularly and protected from thrips and slugs. Its late summer and autumn display can, in some climates and conditions, extend into winter and beyond. The flowers are usually scarlet. It is a dainty plant reaching a height of 24 in (60 cm) and spread of 12 in (30 cm). Several named varieties are available in shades of pink, including the rose pink **'Mrs. Hegarty'**, the salmon pink **'Sunrise'** and the crimson **'Grandiflora'** (syn. 'Gigantea', 'Major'). **'Viscountess Byng'** has pale pink flowers with narrow petals; **'Hilary Gould'** has pink flowers with a stripe-like red marking; and **'Jennifer'** has mid-pink flowers. ZONES 6–10.

SCILLA

Squill, bluebell

This genus of about 90 species of bulbous perennials from Europe, Asia and Africa is dependable for its terminal racemes of usually blue flowers in spring, although they also come in pink, purple and white. Varying from 2 to 20 in (5 to 50 cm) in height, their tiny, usually star-shaped flowers are clustered above strap-shaped leaves. They look good naturalized under trees and shrubs or in lawns.

CULTIVATION Most are adaptable to cold-winter climates and naturalize with ease in lawns and gardens. All should be planted in autumn in average soil in full sun to light shade. Divide in late summer when clumps become crowded, or propagate from seed in autumn.

Scilla peruviana

Scilla peruviana
Cuban lily, wild hyacinth, Peruvian scilla

This plant has a dense cluster of up to 50 star-shaped flowers that are borne in summer on a 12 in (30 cm) long stem. The 1 in (25 mm) wide flowers are usually blue, sometimes white or purple. The dark to olive green foliage is glossy and strap-like. 'Alba' bears white flowers. ZONES 6–10.

Scilla siberica
Siberian squill

In established patches of this Siberian species, rich blue flowers on loose racemes are produced in

Scilla siberica

Scilla verna

such quantity as to color the ground blue. The flowers appear in early to midspring on 6 in (15 cm) stems. The foliage dies soon after flowering finishes. It spreads rapidly by division of bulbs and from seed, and does not do well where winters are mild. 'Spring Beauty' (syn. 'Atrocaerulea') has deep blue flowers and grows to a height of 8 in (20 cm). ZONES 3–9.

Scilla verna
Sea onion, spring scilla

Blunt, concave leaves up to 8 in (20 cm) long appear before the heads of 6 to 12 bluish flowers on this species. The flowerheads are not as tall as the leaves, but the leaves arch away from the flowers so that the blooms are well displayed. ZONES 6–9.

SPARAXIS

Harlequin flower

This is a genus of 6 species of deciduous perennials from South Africa. They have loose spikes of 5 cup-shaped, brightly colored flowers that are borne in spring and summer and look good in raised beds or borders. The leaves are lance-shaped and ribbed and occur in an erect, basal fan. CULTIVATION Grow in moderately fertile, well-drained soil in full sun to light shade and provide shelter from cold winds; in colder areas, they may need greenhouse shelter. Water lightly during growth and not at all when dormant. Propagate from seed or corms.

Sparaxis tricolor
Velvet flower

This marginally frost-hardy native of South Africa is easily grown in warm areas. The 12 in (30 cm) wiry, drooping stems bear a spike of up to 5 funnel-shaped or star-shaped blooms in spring. The 2 in (5 cm) flowers are red to pink or orange, usually with a yellow center outlined in black; they close

Sparaxis tricolor subsp. *blanda*

Sparaxis tricolor

at night and on dull days. **Sparaxis tricolor** subsp. **blanda** is a beautiful, white-flowered version. ZONES 8–10.

STERNBERGIA

Autumn crocus, autumn daffodil

This genus of 8 species of flowering bulbs ranges from Italy across to Iran and was named in honor of botanist Count Kaspar von Sternberg (1761–1838), a founder of the National Museum in Prague.

Sternbergia lutea

They have large, crocus-like flowers that appear in spring or autumn and are related to daffodils.
CULTIVATION They need a hot, sunny site in well-drained soil and should be planted against a sunny wall in cool climates. If left undisturbed they will form clumps. Propagate by division in spring or autumn.

Sternbergia lutea

This delightful species is native to the Mediterranean region. The buttercup yellow flowers are 2 in (5 cm) long and are borne singly on 6 in (15 cm) stems in autumn. The slender leaves are strap-like. It is only just frost hardy and needs warm, dry conditions when dormant in summer; it is best grown in pots in areas with wet summers and makes an excellent plant in a rock garden. ZONES 7–10.

T

TIGRIDIA

Tiger flower

This genus contains about 35 species of cormous plants native to Central and South America. The distinctive flowers inspire admiration for their strikingly spotted centers and 3 bold outer petals in red, orange, pink, yellow, purple or white. They are short lived, usually each lasting only a day, but they make up for this by blooming in succession for weeks during summer.

CULTIVATION Tigridias are subtropical plants but will tolerate light frosts. In cooler areas,

the corms should be lifted and stored during winter or the plants grown in a greenhouse. They need a position in full sun in well-drained soil; water amply in summer. Propagate from seed sown in spring.

Tigridia pavonia
Jockey's cap lily, peacock flower, tiger flower

This Mexican native blooms in summer. The 6 in (15 cm) triangular flowers are usually red with a yellow center spotted with purple, borne on 24 in (60 cm) stems. The foliage is iris-like, sword-shaped and pleated. ZONES 8–10.

TRILLIUM

Wake robin, wood lily, trinity flower

Among North America's most beautiful wildflowers, this genus of the lily family contains 30 species of rhizomatous, deciduous

Tigridia pavonia

Trillium grandiflorum

perennials; they also occur wild in northeastern Asia. Upright or nodding, solitary, funnel-shaped flowers with 3 simple petals are held just above a whorl of 3 leaves. The numerous species are found in woodland habitats, flowering in spring before the appearance of the deciduous leaves, which remain green until autumn. They make good ornamentals in wild gardens and shady borders.
CULTIVATION Very frost hardy, they prefer a cool, moist soil with ample water and shade from the hot afternoon sun. Watch out for mice: they like to eat trilliums in winter. Although slow to propagate from seed in autumn or by division in summer, they are long lived once established.

Trillium grandiflorum
Snow trillium, wake robin

This showy, clump-forming trillium is the easiest to grow, reaching 12–18 in (30–45 cm) in height. The pure white flowers, borne in spring, fade to pink as they age. The double-flowered white form, **'Flore Pleno'**, is beautiful but rare, and has arching stems and oval, dark green leaves. ZONES 3–9.

Trillium sessile
Toad-shade, wake robin

This upright, clump-forming perennial reaches 12–15 in (30–38 cm) in height with a spread of 12–18 in (30–45 cm). It has deep green leaves marbled with pale

Trillium grandiflorum 'Flore Pleno'

Trillium sessile var. *californicum*

green, gray and maroon. They bear stalkless, maroon flowers with lance-shaped petals in late spring. *Trillium sessile* var. *californicum* bears white flowers. ZONES 4–9.

TRITELEIA

The name of this bulb genus of 15 species comes from the Latin "tri," meaning "three parts," and refers to the fact that the flowers are arranged in threes. The genus is closely related to *Brodiaea*, and it is under this name that species are often listed. Most are native to the west coast of North America. They usually produce grass-like foliage, with the onion-like leaves often dying before the flowerheads appear. The well-held umbels of starry flowers, usually borne in late spring, are blue and resemble the *Allium* species.

CULTIVATION These bulbs like moist, well-drained soil, with drier conditions from late summer to early autumn; they should never be waterlogged. Plant where there is full sun for at least part of the day during the growing period. In cold areas, they may need some winter protection. The corms, which should be planted in a sunny but sheltered position in autumn, can be dry-stored during the mid- to late summer dormancy.

Triteleia laxa 'Queen Fabiola'

Triteleia laxa
syn. *Brodiaea laxa*
Grass nut, triplet lily, ithuriel's spur

The showy *Triteleia laxa*, with flowers varying between milky blue and purple-blue, is a popular and easily grown garden plant. It has the largest flower umbels—up to 6 in (15 cm) in diameter—of any species in the genus. The umbels, however, are not as tight as in other species, with flower stalks over 2 in (5 cm) long. The flowers are borne from late spring to early summer; the stems are strong and wiry. 'Queen Fabiola' is a little taller and has even stronger stems. ZONES 7–10.

TULBAGHIA

This is an African genus of 20 rhizomatous, tuberous or cormous perennials. The plants are generally evergreen, with clump-forming,

Tulbaghia violacea 'Silver Lace'

or container, and exudes a garlic-like odor. The flowers range from deep lilac to white and appear sporadically between midspring and late autumn. The narrow, gray-green leaves are more or less evergreen. It is good as a border plant or in a rock garden. The bulbs are edible. **'Silver Lace'** is a variegated form, with leaves edged in white. It is slightly less robust than the species and is believed to be a good mole deterrent. ZONES 7–10.

narrow leaves. The dainty flowers, which are carried in long-stalked umbels, appear spasmodically over a long period during the warmer months. Some species are onion scented; others smell pleasantly of hyacinths.
CULTIVATION These plants withstand moderate frost, provided the drainage is good and there is protection from cold, wet winds. They need full sun and moisture while the foliage is developing; water should be withheld once the flowers appear. Propagate from offsets, which can be removed while the plant is dormant.

Tulbaghia violacea
Society garlic

Robust and clump forming, this plant grows to 30 in (75 cm) in height. It thrives in dry or wet summer climates, in a garden bed

TULIPA

Tulip

Tulips are one of the world's major commercial flower crops, both for cut flowers and horticulture. Wild species of these bulbs come from the eastern Mediterranean. They were introduced into Europe in about 1554 and have been popular ever since. There are more than 100 species of *Tulipa*, but most of those we know are cultivars of only a few species, chiefly *Tulipa*

Useful Tip

As the emerging leaves of tulips begin to unfurl, spray or drench with pyrethrum down the center of the leaf cluster. This will also cover the flower buds and help prevent aphid damage.

gesneriana. Cultivars run into thousands and their names sometimes vary between different countries. Modern revisions of cultivars have led to the present set of 15 groups or divisions. Characteristics are those which are produced in the Royal General Bulbgrowers' Association (KAVB) trial garden in Holland; they are classified according to characteristics such as stem length, flower features and time of flowering. By choosing bulbs from across the groups, you can have a sequence of flowering throughout spring. They range in height from 4 in (10 cm) to 27 in (70 cm). The blooms come in many colors, including bronze, black, yellow, white, red, pink, purple, violet, green and blue. CULTIVATION Climate crucially affects tulip flowering; they require dry, warm summers but cold winters. Plant in late autumn, preferably in a sunny position, in deep, rich, preferably alkaline, well-drained soil. In warmer climates chill the bulbs for 4 to 8 weeks prior to planting. Water well during their growth period. Deadhead the flowers as they fade unless you want seed or species to set, but allow leaves to die off naturally in order to replenish the bulb. In areas with wet summers, lift bulbs and store under cool, dry conditions. Tulips are prone to

Tulipa clusiana var. *chrysantha*

aphid attack and the fungal disease tulip fire, which thrives under moist conditions. Propagate from offsets or seed in autumn.

Tulipa clusiana
syn. *Tulipa aitchisonii, T. stellata*
Lady tulip, peppermint stick tulip

One of the most graceful of all tulips, this lovely species produces elegant, star-like flowers, white inside with a violet base and outer tepals which are carmine on the outside. They grow to about 10 in (25 cm) tall and require minimal chilling, making them a delightful

Tulipa cultivar

Tulipa saxatilis

T., Single Early Group, 'Beauty Queen'

lasting garden plant, even in milder climates. Occasionally more than one flower per stem is produced. ***Tulipa clusiana*** var. ***chrysantha*** (syn. *T. chrysantha*) is smaller than *T. clusiana*, reaching only 8 in (20 cm) in height, but its small flowers, deep yellow inside, are long, slim and elegant in bud. The outer petals may have a yellow edge. ZONES 5–9.

Tulipa saxatilis
syn. *Tulipa bakeri*

This very showy species was first described in 1825, in Crete. It reaches a height of 8 in (20 cm) and usually produces 2 cups per stem; they are rosy lilac with yellow bases. Minimal chilling requirements make it very easy to grow and suitable for naturalizing, although deep planting is advisable. It spreads by underground stolons, rarely sets seed and has very glossy, fresh green leaves which often appear in late autumn and make it through the winter unmarked. Its slightly smaller cultivar, **'Lilac Wonder'**, has an exterior of pinkish purple, the inner ring of petals being somewhat

Tulipa saxatilis 'Lilac Wonder'

T., Triumph Group, Garden Party cultivar

Tulipa, Darwin Hybrid Group, 'Apeldoorn'

Tulipa, Darwin Hybrid Group, 'Oxford'

lighter, and a pale yellow base. The interior is pastel mauve with a large, circular, lemon yellow base and yellow anthers. It grows to only 6 in (15 cm). ZONES 5–9.

Tulipa cultivars

The **Single Early Group** has single-flowered cultivars, generally short stemmed and mostly deriving from *Tulipa gesneriana*. Popular examples of these early-flowering tulips include **'Apricot Beauty'**, **'Beauty Queen'** and **'Keizerskroon'** (syn. 'Grand Duc').

The **Double Early Group** contains mainly short-stemmed, double, early-flowering cultivars which resemble gardenias. **'Monte Carlo'**, **'Murillo'**, **'Peach Blossom'** and **'Yellow Baby'** are good examples of this group.

The **Triumph Group** has single-flowered cultivars with medium-length stems that flower mid-season. A feature of many of these is flowers with edgings or markings in a contrasting color. Popular cultivars include **'Abu Hassan'**, **'Garden Party'**, **'Merry Widow'** and **'Rosario'**.

The **Darwin Hybrid Group** consists of the single-flowered, long-stemmed cultivars that flower mid-season. They are the most frequently grown varieties for the cut-flower market. **'Apeldoorn'**, **'Golden Apeldoorn'**, **'Gudoshnik'**, **'Oxford'** and **'Golden Oxford'** are all excellent cultivars.

Useful Tip

For a one-year show of spring bulbs in a warm climate, buy bulbs and chill them for 8 to 10 weeks in a refrigerator before planting. Aim to plant at the coolest time of year.

T., Single Late Group, 'Clara Butt'

T., Single Late Group, 'Queen of Night'

The **Single Late Group** comprises single, late-flowering, mainly long-stemmed cultivars including '**Clara**

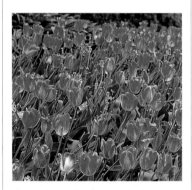

T., Single Late Group, 'Dreamland'

Butt', '**Dreamland**', '**Grand Style**' and '**Queen of Night**'; the latter is one of the very best of the "black" tulips available.

The **Lily-flowered Group** of single-flowered cultivars blooms in mid- or late season. The flowers form a star on opening and have stems of variable length. Examples include '**Ballade**', '**Lilac Time**' and '**Red Shine**'.

The **Fringed Group** of single-flowered cultivars have petals edged with crystal-shaped fringes. They flower mid- or late season

T., Single Late Group, 'Grand Style'

Tulipa, Lily-flowered Group, 'Lilac Time'

Tulipa, Lily-flowered Group, 'Red Shine'

Tulipa, Parrot Group, 'Flaming Parrot'

and stems are of variable length. 'Aleppo', 'Fringed Beauty' and 'Redwing' are popular.

The **Viridiflora Group** are late-flowering single-flowered cultivars of variable stem length and partly greenish tepals. The muted 'Spring Green' is popular.

The **Parrot Group** consists of unusually-colored cultivars with curled or twisted petals. They are mainly late flowering and stem lengths vary. 'Apricot Parrot' and 'Flaming Parrot' are examples.

The **Double Late Group** (or Peony-flowered) contains late-flowering, mainly long-stemmed cultivars, similar to those of the Parrot Group. 'Granda' and 'Angelique' are among the most popular.

The **Kaufmanniana Group** is very early-flowering. The blooms, with a multi-colored base and an exterior which normally has a clear carmine blush, open fully and reach a height of up to 8 in (20 cm). The foliage is sometimes mottled. Cultivars include 'Giuseppe Verdi', 'Heart's Delight' and 'Shakespeare'.

Tulipa, Fringed Group, 'Fringed Beauty'

Tulipa, Double Late Group, 'Angelique'

Tulipa, Greigii Group, 'Oriental Splendour'

Tulipa, Greigii Group, 'Red Riding Hood'

The **Fosteriana Group** has the most brilliant of all tulips. Early flowering, the leaves are very broad, green or gray-green, sometimes mottled or striped. Stems are medium to long and they have large, long flowers with variable bases. 'Golden Eagle' is a vivid combination of yellow and orange with a dark orange exterior, while

'**Robassa**' is red, with a yellow base and cream edges.

The **Greigii Group** cultivars have large flowers of variable shape. Heights too are variable, but generally in the middle ranges. Cultivars include '**Oriental Splendour**', '**Plaisir**', '**Red Riding Hood**' and '**Sweet Lady**', the latter being one of the most delightfully colored in the group, being a pinkish orange with a base of bronzy green, tinged yellow. Its mottled leaves add to its interest. ZONES 5–9.

Tulipa, Greigii Group, 'Plaisir'

Tulipa, Greigii Group, 'Sweet Lady'

WZ

WATSONIA

This genus of about 60 species of cormous perennials is native to South Africa and Madagascar. Their spikes of fragrant, tubular, red, orange, pink or white flowers resemble gladioli, although they are somewhat more tubular in form. Flowers usually appear from spring to summer. The leaves are also similar to those of gladioli, being sword-shaped and erect. There are evergreen and deciduous species available.

Watsonia pillansii

CULTIVATION The corms should be planted in autumn in light, well-drained soil in a sunny spot. In cold areas, it is best to plant in pots to overwinter in a frost-free greenhouse or conservatory. In spring, sink the pots in the ground or plant them out in summer. Lift in autumn in cold areas. Clumps are best left undisturbed and allowed to spread freely. Propagate from seed in the autumn or by division if clumps become too overcrowded.

Watsonia pillansii
syn. *Watsonia beatricis*
Beatrice watsonia

This evergreen species grows to 4 ft (1.2 m) in height. The flower spike bears salmon pink, tubular, star-shaped flowers 3 in (8 cm) long in late summer to autumn. The green foliage is sword shaped. Hardier than other species, it can withstand some frost. A number of hybrids have been developed from this species, including

'Watermelon Shades', and there is some doubt about whether this plant, common in nurseries under this name, is the true wild species. ZONES 7–10.

ZANTEDESCHIA

Calla lily

Indigenous to southern and eastern Africa, this well-known genus

Zantedeschia aethiopica

of the arum family consists of 6 species of tuberous perennials. The inflorescence consists of a showy white, yellow or pink spathe shaped like a funnel, with a central finger-like, yellow spadix. The leaves are glossy green and usually arrowhead-shaped.

CULTIVATION Consisting of both evergreen and deciduous species, this genus includes frost-tender to moderately frost-hardy plants. Most are intolerant of dry conditions, preferring well-drained soil in full sun or part-shade, although *Zantedeschia aethiopica* will grow as a semi-aquatic plant in boggy ground. Propagate from offsets in winter.

Zantedeschia aethiopica
White arum lily, lily of the Nile

Although normally deciduous, in summer and early autumn this species can stay evergreen if given enough moisture. It can also be grown in water up to 6–12 in (15–30 cm) deep. *Zantedeschia aethiopica* reaches 24–36 in

(60–90 cm) in height and spread, with large clumps of broad, dark green leaves. The large flowers, produced in spring, summer and autumn, are pure white with a striking yellow spadix. '**Crowborough**' is more cold tolerant and better suited to cool climates, such as the UK and the northwest USA. It grows to about 3 ft (1 m) tall. '**Green Goddess**' has interesting green markings on the spathes. ZONES 8–11.

Zantedeschia aethiopica 'Crowborough'

Zantedeschia aethiopica 'Green Goddess'

HARDINESS ZONE MAPS

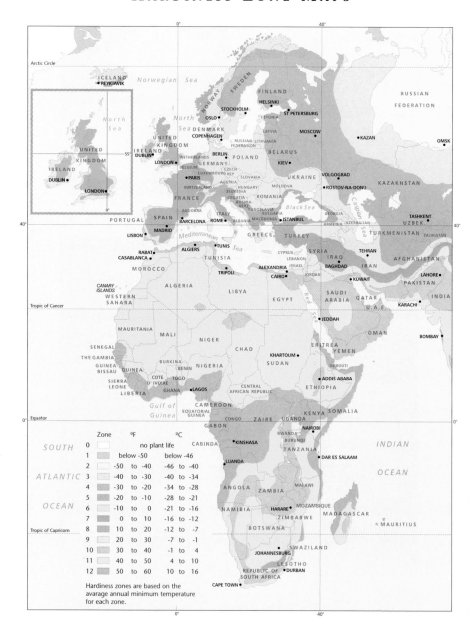

Zone	°F	°C
0	no plant life	no plant life
1	below -50	below -46
2	-50 to -40	-46 to -40
3	-40 to -30	-40 to -34
4	-30 to -20	-34 to -28
5	-20 to -10	-28 to -21
6	-10 to 0	-21 to -16
7	0 to 10	-16 to -12
8	10 to 20	-12 to -7
9	20 to 30	-7 to -1
10	30 to 40	-1 to 4
11	40 to 50	4 to 10
12	50 to 60	10 to 16

Hardiness zones are based on the
avarage annual minimum temperature
for each zone.

Note: The scale of this map differs from that of the following two maps.

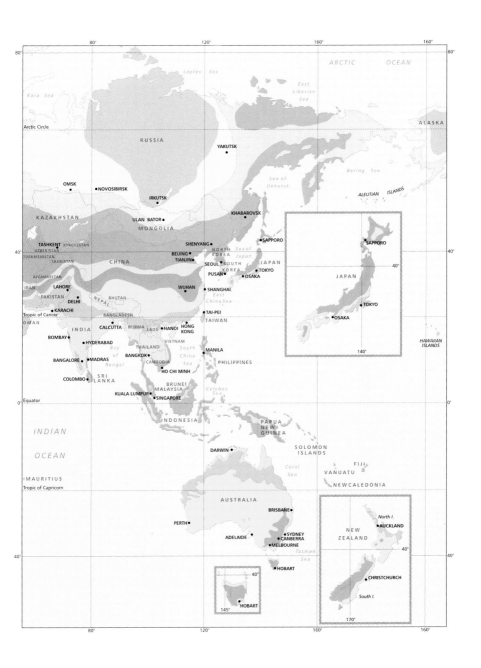

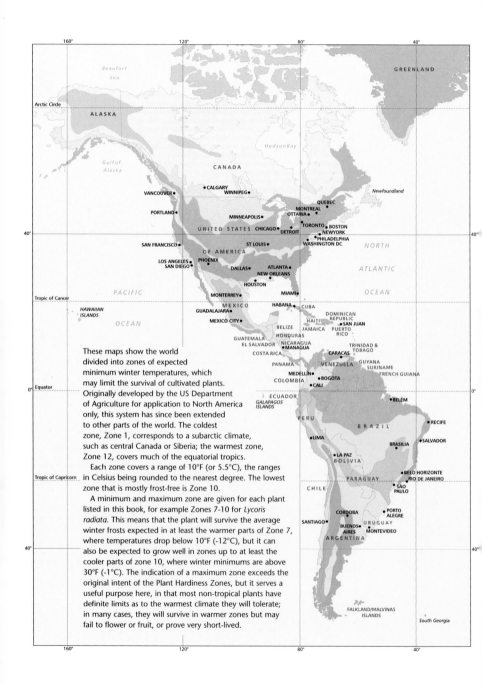

These maps show the world divided into zones of expected minimum winter temperatures, which may limit the survival of cultivated plants. Originally developed by the US Department of Agriculture for application to North America only, this system has since been extended to other parts of the world. The coldest zone, Zone 1, corresponds to a subarctic climate, such as central Canada or Siberia; the warmest zone, Zone 12, covers much of the equatorial tropics.

Each zone covers a range of 10°F (or 5.5°C), the ranges in Celsius being rounded to the nearest degree. The lowest zone that is mostly frost-free is Zone 10.

A minimum and maximum zone are given for each plant listed in this book, for example Zones 7-10 for *Lycoris radiata*. This means that the plant will survive the average winter frosts expected in at least the warmer parts of Zone 7, where temperatures drop below 10°F (-12°C), but it can also be expected to grow well in zones up to at least the cooler parts of zone 10, where winter minimums are above 30°F (-1°C). The indication of a maximum zone exceeds the original intent of the Plant Hardiness Zones, but it serves a useful purpose here, in that most non-tropical plants have definite limits as to the warmest climate they will tolerate; in many cases, they will survive in warmer zones but may fail to flower or fruit, or prove very short-lived.

INDEX